The Farmhouse
Elizabeth Bromke

THE FARMHOUSE

Published by:

Elizabeth Bromke

White Mountains, Arizona

For Dorothy

Chapter 1 — Maggie

Maggie Engel stared blankly at the fresh, white stack of pages on the table in front of her.

It all seemed so simple. *Too* simple.

"Who knew you could print out a divorce?" she joked.

Becky shrugged. "You still have to appear in court. That's what I did with Andrew."

"Did you print the paperwork first?" Maggie pushed the packet away and rose from her chair to check on Becky's foils. "Ten more minutes then we rinse, by the way."

Her best friend adjusted the magazine on her lap. "My divorce was almost twenty years ago. Things were different. You had to duke it out in person then drive to the courthouse *with him*. You had to sit there, sobbing like a wretched housewife while he white-knuckled the steering wheel in painful silence. No hiding behind a computer screen. No surprises. No printing." Becky lifted a folded foil from her face to take a sip of her tea. "I can't believe I have gray hairs sprouting up. Is this what happens after forty? The clock starts ticking?"

"For some, yeah. Not me." It was meant to be playful, but Maggie's voice came out flat and lifeless. She could use a gray hair or two. As long as they came with the wisdom she'd been desperately lacking most of her adult life.

Maggie moved the paperwork to the island and prepped her kitchen sink for shampooing.

Becky scooted the chair back from the table, its rubber stoppers scuffing the linoleum floor in little, black smears, like rubbed-off mascara. "You're lucky, Mags. I don't know why you bleach your hair when you have that vibrant, natural red."

"Blondes have more fun, right? At least, that's what they told me. Seems to be a big, fat lie, though." Maggie recalled using the same stale response the year before, when she and Becky reunited in the Linden family home down the hill past Main Street.

After almost two decades living in Arizona, Maggie's best friend found the freedom to return home to Hickory Grove. All it took was 18 years of single-momming and then, voila—Becky's son did the same thing that most well-raised children did. He packed and left for college.

Scrubbing a dried Cheerio from the back corner of the sink reminded Maggie that she, herself, had about fourteen years left until the last of her brood was out of the house. Did she have to wait that long for a fresh start, too?

"When did you know it was over with Andrew?" she asked Becky, drying her hands on her apron.

A frown took hold of Becky's mouth. "Immediately. I wouldn't have married him, actually. But then, well, *Theo...*" her voice trailed off and she flipped the page. It was the only tattered reading material Maggie had on hand—a July 2016 edition of *Hearth and Home*.

Outside the bay window overlooking Pine Tree Lane, tiny white flakes were floating down onto the front lawn. Travis never did mow the grass back in October, at the end of a long, dry fall. But, Maggie did. She gave those tall, weedy blades a good, old-fashioned buzz cut.

The fresh snowflakes ought to be thankful they didn't have to fight their way through weeds down to the earth. Instead, they settled neatly atop of the crunchy, yellowy yard. If the clouds promised to hang around, maybe a pretty sheet of frosting would blanket Maggie's unadorned property in a stretch of brilliant white.

Maggie swallowed over the stubborn lump that had formed at the base of her throat, but it would not go down.

"Yeah, but you don't regret having your *son*," Maggie pointed out, checking Becky's roots.

Becky waved a hand. "Obviously I don't regret having Theo. But Andrew and I weren't soul mates. I mean, are you and *Travis* soul mates? Was Gretchen a love child or a surprise?" Becky asked, rhetorically. Maggie wasn't a prude, and she loved a good joke, but she wasn't laughing at the fact that both of them wound up pregnant so soon after high school and with men who fell so short of their expectations and hopes and dreams.

Maggie recalled that Gretchen cracked her first smile the same day Becky called her and announced the news. The day was vivid in her mind. Happy tears coursed down both twenty-year-olds' faces and made for an intermittently silent phone call. Silent sobs. And, an awkwardness had stilted the conversation the women managed to push through the line. But by the time the news was over, each was happy for herself and for the other. Subsequent conversations grew giddy with excitement. Eventually, they chatted loftily, wondering if their babies would one day grow up together. Become best friends. Maybe

Becky would have a boy—she did—and they would get married. Becky and Maggie could be mothers-in-law together.

Becky turned and propped her elbow on the table. "You don't want to leave him, do you?"

The women locked eyes for a brief moment until Maggie shook her head and dabbed along her lower lash line with the pads of her pinkies. Black eyeliner smudged beneath her fake nails.

She glanced at her reflection in the microwave above the stove, and though it wasn't a clear picture, Maggie saw how she looked.

Like a clown.

She looked like a dang clown. A laugh escaped her lips and all of a sudden she was cracking up—laughing so hard she was crying. Crying so hard she was laughing. It was a chicken-or-the-egg type of situation.

Becky stared at her friend, lifting the foil panels. This served, of course, to make Maggie laugh harder. The tears were wipe-awayable now. "You look as ridiculous as me," she snorted through a final, shuddering sob.

"Oh, Maggie, it will be okay." Becky stood and wrapped her friend in a hug.

"Let's get you to the sink." Maggie sniffled herself back together and then guided Becky to bend her head into the sink.

It wasn't a glamorous set up, Maggie's in-home salon. But it was as functional as she could make it.

After tucking a second towel around Becky's neck, Maggie began to tug the foils loose, one by one, balling them up and tossing them in the nearby trash. Finally, she turned the faucet on cool and began running her fingers through Becky's long, chestnut strands, her nails clacking against the inside walls of her kitchen sink.

"Is this comfortable enough?" Maggie asked, turning the faucet warmer as she pumped a dollop of shampoo into her palm.

"Not comfortable, but I'm fine," Becky answered, her voice echoing in the basin as she shifted her weight and pressed her hands against the sink.

Sometimes, Maggie wished she worked in a real salon with a real shampoo station. But then she remembered how much she longed for a change of pace. Beauty school, for Maggie, had only been a back-up plan. It was not her first choice. In fact, much of Maggie's life had turned into something of a back-up plan. So much so that she wasn't quite sure what her first choice ever was. Or if she even had one.

Suds foamed between her fingers as Maggie massaged Becky's scalp from the base to the hairline along her forehead and then rinsed.

"Mmmm," Becky cooed from beneath. Maggie finished rinsing and pulled a fresh-from-the-dryer towel from her caddy and wrapped Becky's head in it.

Once back at the table, Maggie tousled and patted until her friend's newly colored locks were no longer sopping. She pulled a strand forward and showed it to Becky. "See? No more grays. Just warm, maple tones."

Becky twisted the hair around her finger and lifted her eyebrows. "You are the best hair stylist I've ever had. Seriously, Mags," Becky continued. "You're wasting your talent in Hickory Grove."

With an eye roll for an answer, Maggie hooked a comb into Becky's wet hair and pulled mercilessly.

Becky squirmed but didn't whine, and Maggie apologized for being a little rough. "I do want to leave him, you know. I *will* leave him."

"Good. You need to. Travis is a cheating brute of a man. And in fact..." Becky twisted in her chair, resting her hand on Maggie's arm to keep her from combing. "If you don't leave him, then I'm placing a phone call."

Maggie frowned, and a pit broke open in her stomach. She felt herself grow hot, and guilt crawled up her throat, turning, briefly, to nausea. Her kids. She knew Becky's number one concern was Maggie's own kids. Not Maggie or the heartbreak she'd endured for years.

"What do you mean?" Maggie asked, sweat breaking out on her lower back despite the chill that crept in through a crack in the molding of the window.

"If you don't fill out that paperwork and *follow through* this time, then I'm calling Dirk."

Maggie blew out a sigh. "I can assure you that calling my brother will result in nothing more than childish threats against Travis's tires or a plot to go meet him in a back alley. Besides, Dirk is on a rig right now. Won't be back for months."

It was true. As he had throughout high school, Maggie's twin brother would promise to break Travis's neck. And, if Dirk *were* in town, that threat would result in a fumbling brawl behind the Hickory Grove Alehouse. If she was *lucky*. "Leave Dirk out of it. Travis is my mess. Not my brother's."

"That might be true," Becky pointed out, just before Maggie grabbed the blow dryer and a round brush. "But Travis has also become your kids' mess. Maybe it's time for you to clean house."

Chapter 2 — Rhett

Rhett Houston shook his head at the man in coveralls whose clean hands belied the messy work of a mechanic. Grease-free nail beds were a bad sign, but Rhett didn't have any other options at the time. It was just as well, anyway.

A confrontation with Travis Engel was long coming.

"I don't want you to change the *oil,* Trav. I can do that myself. All I need is the one new tire."

He began to wonder if his return to Hickory Grove was a mistake. Granted, this was Rhett's second foul experience so far, the first being his blown out tire on the highway.

Naw. He could handle one shoddy mechanic. Especially if that man was his former high school nemesis. Rhett wasn't the sort to gloat and hold his own personal accomplishments over loser punks who never lived up to their potential.

Then again, did Travis Engel have any potential to begin with?

"All right, Houston. Come back in a couple hours. We'll give her a work up, *and* you can have a friends-and-family discount." The slick-talking jerk spat into a plastic tumbler and set it on the desk before tossing Rhett's keys to the other guy who'd been hanging around in the door frame that connected the cigarette-stained office to the cluttered garage. Rhett glanced at the latter and realized all the grit that belonged under Travis's fingernails and between the wrinkles in his knuckles had wound up on the other guy. His whole face was a shade of putrid gray, and if he would just run his fingers through his hair, he'd at least *look* the part of a greaser.

Rhett nodded and left without a word. Travis didn't owe him squat. Not a discount. Not anything. And had he known the jerk still ran the only garage in town, he would have had his truck towed back into Louisville. His king cab, four-wheel-drive baby popped like a firecracker on the Hickory Grove end of the Ohio River, and Rhett was forced to have it (and himself) hauled five miles into his destination.

Zipping his jacket up to his neck, the forty-year-old stepped off Hickory Grove Automotive's icy front curb and crossed the traffic-free Main Street. Now *this* he missed.

Louisville was a bumper-to-bumper warzone of commuters and business types, families, and tourists. It had everything and nothing. Rhett enjoyed the money he'd made there, but not the time and energy-suck of living in a big city. Or the vapid women he'd attracted.

A purposeful stride turned into a leisurely walk as Rhett took in the sights along Hickory Grove's main drag. In fifteen years, not much had changed.

The bank still took up the corner lot. Next to it, the Ice Cream Shoppe. Across, were a couple of boutiques and then Mally's, the town hub.

Every Saturday night, after little league or a basketball tournament or whatever sport Rhett was playing at the time, his parents would bring him and his little sister, Greta, to Mally's. They'd order breakfast-for-dinner, Rhett's favorite. It was a far cry from suppers at home. Their mom always had a formal meal waiting—something severe and Dutch or fanciful and French. Never pancakes. Adele Houston's heritage clung to her right up until Greta graduated from high school, at which point the Houston family matriarch convinced her husband to move back to her hometown in Pennsylvania, to be near her parents in their final years.

And that's where they had stayed.

Rhett swung open the door to Mally's with gusto, cringing as the old bell clanged to life, announcing his arrival. Though he was excited for buttermilk hotcakes, he wasn't looking to draw attention to himself.

"Sorry about that," he offered the brassy, blonde, bubblegum-popping waitress behind the counter. "Is Mally in?" Slushy snow soaked into the ragged utility mat, and Rhett tried discreetly to knock off the rest of the melting crystals.

She snapped her gum and frowned. "He's dead."

Rhett's chest burned at the curt reply, and he shoved his hands into his pockets, feeling awkward at receiving news that wasn't quite personal but that hit like a mini heart attack. "I'm real sorry to hear that," he replied, his eyes darting around the place. It was mostly as he'd remembered. A dated diner that never hosted more than a handful of patrons.

"Wanna take a seat?" the girl asked, rounding the counter and striding toward the hostess stand where she pulled out a grimy, plastic menu and pushed it toward him, apparently new and unaware of the proper order of events.

His gaze still darting around as he measured the restaurant's changes, he sighed at last. "Sure."

Rhett followed the teenager to a window booth, and as he slid onto the bouncing plastic, she rattled off the specials, concluding with the soup of the day. He looked up from the menu and locked eyes with her for the first time since getting his bearings.

Rhett blinked. "Wow," he breathed, his mouth agape. "You're a dead ringer for..."

"Listen here, buster. If you think you can waltz into *my* town and *hit* on me like a walking mid-life crisis, well then—"

Rhett held up his hands in a panic. "No, no, no. No," he interrupted, his neck flushing up to his ears. "I didn't mean that at all. It's just..."

"Spit it out, bud." She snapped her gum and rolled her eyes, crossing her arms beneath her name tag. *Gretchen E.*

"You're... you're *Maggie Devereux's* daughter!" It hit him like a sack of bricks, and everything about his unsuspecting waitress fell into place. Her thick twang and sassy attitude. The red streaks peeking out from brassy highlights. A smattering of freckles across her nose and cheeks.

The girl's mouth dropped open, and her gum nearly fell onto the tabletop. "You mean *Engel*?" she asked, resuming her composure, tucking her gum into one cheek, and then giving him a hard stare.

Rhett swallowed. "Engel?"

"My mother is Maggie *Engel*." She tapped the little *E.* on her nametag and lifted an auburn eyebrow.

Shaking his head, he tried for a fresh start. "I'm sorry. My name is Rhett. I graduated from Hickory Grove High with Maggie *Devereux*. Is that your mom?"

"Yeah. Well, it's who she *used* to be."

A headache began to set in at the base of his skull, but Rhett replied evenly. "That's right. She married him." The waitress cocked her head at his confusion. "Travis Engel, I mean."

"Look, it's cool that you're on some sort of vacation down memory lane, but I'm on the clock." She tipped her chin toward a huddle of coats waiting by the front door.

Rhett nodded and ordered a coffee, black, before the girl flashed a saccharin grin and tucked her pen behind her ear. "Be right back with that coffee, Mr. Rhett. And, uh, sorry for thinking you were..."

Rhett waved off her apology and settled into the booth, studying the menu and feeling disappointed to learn that Mally's—which, by now, he figured really ought to change its name—no longer served breakfast all day long.

"All right, what'll it be, Mr. Rhett?" Gretchen had reappeared, a fresh smile replacing the earlier, forced one.

He cleared his throat. "You can just call me Rhett. And I'll take a burger, I suppose. Plain. No cheese."

"Burger and coffee? That's a new one." She chuckled, and Rhett's stomach twisted into knots at the bizarre reminder of his old friend. He knew Maggie had kids. But it still felt surreal. Maggie was a mom. A mom of a teenager, at the least. Maybe even a young woman.

Slowly closing the menu, he offered it to her and pointed out the obvious. "You sound exactly like your mom."

"I get that a lot," Gretchen answered, earnestly, as she jotted down his simple order and took the menu. "Be right back with your burger." She strode away, and Rhett watched the front door swing open once more, undermining his previous assumption that business must have died off when Mally did.

The new arrival's face was unfamiliar and his age hard to peg. He could have been fifteen or twenty-five.

Rhett watched on as Maggie's daughter pranced over to him and flirted, confirming Rhett's suspicions about the adolescent shape to the boy's face.

Moments later, after the girl and the customer flounced just past him, Rhett found himself face to face with the boy, who was far friendlier than his waitress friend—or girlfriend, as the case seemed to be. She had sat him in the booth just beyond his, and as Gretchen left to fill his drink order, Rhett met the boy's gaze.

He offered a smile and a nod and tried, unsuccessfully to focus on the muted news that was projecting from the small, mounted tube television above the bar.

Gretchen returned with his hamburger, and—to his surprise and confusion—made small talk.

"So are you just back for a visit?" she asked, while Rhett pushed his French fries to the far corner of his plate.

"Oh," he began, "Sort of. I plan to move back permanently in a few months, but I need to sign some paperwork today. My family owns land out past the old schoolhouse. And, anyway, I have a sister who lives in New Albany and wanted to be closer to her." He felt himself rambling and took a bite of the burger to stop.

"Closer than where?" she asked, leaning her hip into his table.

"Louisville," he replied, wondering if Maggie had ever mentioned him to her friends. He realized that might be awkward and shook the thought. "Anyway, I like small towns better." It felt like a weak justification, and Rhett began to wonder why,

exactly, he *had* chosen Hickory Grove rather than, say Corydon, or Elizabethtown, or *anywhere*. Oh yeah. The Houston
family acres. Seventy five of them, to be exact. The perfect tract
for a hunting cabin or a family home or whatever it was that
Rhett would decide to build. He'd commute back to Louisville
as needed to check on his various rentals. Maybe he'd even pick
up a few properties in Hickory Grove, eventually.

Satisfied that she'd accomplished something, though what
he did not know, the waitress smiled and glanced over to the
boy before trotting off, her steps lighter than before.

"Why Hickory Grove?" the voice belonged to the boy,
whose earnest expression was a mismatch for his female friend's
hot and cold behavior. In that way, she was decidedly *unlike* her
mother.

Rhett sucked in a breath before replying across the booth.
"I'm from here, originally."

"Family still here?" The kid's accent didn't belong. He must
be a west coast transplant. Rhett thought to ask why *he* was in
Hickory Grove, but decided against it. He was growing tired
and needed to get to the lawyer's office to have the deed transferred in his name before heading back into the city in a hopefully functioning truck.

"No, like I said. Sister up north. Parents moved east. But
I've a claim to some land here, and that's what I want. Plus,
friends." The last note was an exaggeration. Maggie never did
reply to his text that he was heading back to town. And Luke,
the very reason he'd even considered buying land in his hometown, was away on business.

Rhett took another bite of his burger but felt the kid's eyes on him. He chewed carefully, then swallowed, wiped his mouth, and threw the guy a bone. "How about you?"

"I'm from Tucson. But my mom grew up here like you. Becky Linden, you know her?"

A cough tickled the back of Rhett's throat, and he put the pieces together. Maggie's daughter became friends with Becky's son. He cleared it and grinned. "Of course I know Becky." He smiled and gestured the kid to join him in his booth. "Rhett Houston." He stuck out his hand.

The boy accepted it and shook it hard. "Theo Linden."

"So your mom is back in Hickory Grove, too?"

"Yep. Moved here in August when I left for college. Notre Dame." The kid beamed.

Rhett pulled a serious face and complimented the impressive detail. "Very nice. So what are you doing around these parts, then?"

Theo smiled past Rhett then dropped his voice. "I'm in love."

A chuckle escaped the older man's mouth and he forced himself not to turn and peer at the feisty waitress. Theo didn't seem to mind though.

"With, uh, Gretchen?" Rhett confirmed.

Nodding gravely, Theo kept mum while the girl in question refilled their drinks and plopped a pile of french fries onto the tabletop. "There ya go," she added, propping her hands on her hips, a smirk dancing across her mouth. "Can I get you anything else? A bottle of wine? Candles?"

Though her joke caught him off guard, Rhett bust into a hearty laughter. Theo, however, flushed deep red, unsure how to reply smoothly.

"If Mally's is still the only place to take a date, then I guess Hickory Grove hasn't changed too much," he said, wiping his mouth as his laugh died off.

Gretchen grinned and shook her head. "I wouldn't know. I don't date."

A silence filled the table at that, and Rhett caught her glance off, avoiding the flash of disappointment apparent on Theo's face.

"I'll take the check," Rhett answered.

THEY'D WRAPPED UP THE awkward lunch and stepped silently into the blustery January day together, as though they'd known each other forever. Theo mentioned he was heading back to school in a week, and Rhett nodded in reply, wondering how the two got hooked up in the first place. Was it Maggie or Becky? He had a feeling it was neither. Maybe just chance.

"Nice to meet you," Theo offered and held out his hand.

Rhett shook it, and replied in kind. "Have a safe drive up-state."

Before the kid took off toward the parking lot, Rhett stopped him. "Oh, and Theo. Before you leave town, you should tell her."

The kid's face scrunched in confusion, and Rhett felt older than his forty years. Like a wizened grandpa coaching a promising shortstop. He began to shake his head as if to leave it alone, but something tugged at his insides. "Maggie's daughter. Gretchen. You should tell her if you like her. Trust me on this."

A bright smile opened on Theo's face, and he shuddered—either from cold or excitement, Rhett couldn't tell. "Yeah, you're right. I should. Thanks, Mr. Houston. Maybe I'll see you around town."

Rhett shook his head. "I'm heading to the city tonight. Won't be here for good until I build my house."

"If you need a place to stay the night or whatever, we have an extra room at my grandparents' house down the hill."

A frigid wind whipped down the sidewalk and nearly knocked the two men into each other. Rhett smiled at the boy's innocent kindness, but said no. "I appreciate that, but I've got a home in the city." What he didn't add was that although the home in question was the one he'd shared with his girlfriend of five years, it was the last place he wanted to be. But Rhett would rather fiddle his thumbs in a motel room than impose.

"Well, if you change your mind, we're just down Main Street past—"

Rhett cracked a wry smile and held up his hand. "I know where the Linden farm is. Small town, remember?"

It was true. He knew Hickory Grove like the back of his hand. The Linden Farm. The schoolhouse and its undeveloped acres beyond. He knew he could walk down to Durbin Family Law Offices if he had a mind to. He knew Travis Engel wouldn't have his tire fixed for at least a few more hours, because he *knew* Hickory Grove.

But, after the strange lunch he'd just finished, none of his previously scheduled business seemed to matter as much.

Because as he pulled his phone from his jeans pocket, a text flashed on the screen.

It was the reply he'd been waiting for.

His old friend. Maggie Devereux.

Chapter 3 — Gretchen

The cafe closed at three o'clock on Mondays, so Gretchen left soon after Theo and the man who knew her mother.

It occurred to her that she could have asked Theo to wait. And he would have waited. But that would be weird.

So instead, Gretchen found herself walking home through the mid-winter afternoon.

In November, when snow felt like a foreigner, she welcomed it—cuddling up in the deepest corner of her twin bed with her ear buds firmly planted and a good mystery book crooked in her hands.

But Christmas had passed and so had the welcome newness of cold weather. It was the first day Gretchen's younger siblings had returned to school after winter break, and in a week, she—like Theo—would be returning to school, too. Though her education was different than his.

Hickory Grove Community College.

The esthetician program.

Gretchen's destiny, apparently.

Her mom had pushed her to it, of course. But what Gretchen really wanted was another life. Not more prestige; nothing like Notre Dame or whatever. But, a quiet life.

Chatting above fumes all day might, in fact, be Gretchen's worst nightmare.

Then again, when her mother asked her point blank what, exactly, she planned to do once she'd graduated from high school, Gretchen came up empty.

Checking the clock on her phone, the eighteen-year-old calculated she had less than an hour until the school bus wheezed its way up Pine Tree Lane, braking like a locomotive in front of her house, and deposited Ky and Dakota onto their front walkway. Little Briar would still be at Mamaw Engel's house, and would remain there until Maggie was finished with appointments or errands for the afternoon.

Gretchen treaded carefully up the icy sidewalk until she came to her street, and by then she'd begun to sweat beneath her coat. She unzipped it and let the frigid air curl inside and wrap its way up her spine, all the while wondering if her mother was home working or out helping Miss Becky, who was still getting the old schoolhouse back on its feet.

On the one hand, Gretchen would have loved even just thirty minutes of girl talk with her mom. On the other, she'd like to enjoy the new book she had checked out just the day before.

The decision was settled when she arrived at her family's two-story home to glimpse a pink piece of paper taped onto the door. Her phone buzzed, distracting her from the errant note—probably an advertisement for snow removal— and she opened the front door, stepping inside and out of the cold air.

Gretchen answered the phone call, only to learn it was an advertisement of a different sort: a spammy robo-caller offering student loan recompense. She clicked it off and took a deep breath in to learn her mother was not, in fact, home. The absence of hair dye fumes or the putrid vapors of a perm proved as much.

So, she tucked into her bedroom at the end of the second floor hall and closed the door before shedding her waitress uniform and bra and pulling on an oversized pair of sweatpants and a hoodie. Then, with the pleasure of a woman who'd been on her feet all day, she fell into bed and grabbed the book that had tangled itself among her unmade bed sheets.

Sewing for Idiots.

It was a departure. No murder. No violence. No whodunnit. But there was a mystery to uncover, and that was how to begin down the path she'd always been curious about. Ever since her Great-Great Aunt Marguerite had passed away just months before.

Gretchen's mother had long poo-pooed the profession. *It's cheaper to shop online than make your own clothes*, she'd often admonished. That much was true, but it didn't change Gretchen's desperate interest in her late aunt's mainstay of so many decades.

Marguerite Devereux, who took the nickname *Lorna* in her latter years, was the go-to seamstress until her passing. Once her apprentice, Miss Patsy, left town, it was like a hole opened up in Hickory Grove. No one to hem a prom dress that fell half an inch too long. No one to shore up the fit of a hand-me-down suit. No one to sell delicately embroidered dish towels with a little white tag pinned onto them which read *Crafted locally*.

Just as she began to concentrate on Chapter One: "Getting Ready to Sew," her phone chirped to life. Gretchen shifted her eyes to its screen, debating whether to give her time to the messenger or to her studies.

In true teenage form, she opted for the former, despite guilt gnawing at her heart. It was always a better decision to ignore the message and read the book, after all.

A text from Theo flashed in green. *Did you make it home? :)*

She sighed and tapped out a curt response. *Yes.* Then, after a beat, decided to add a follow-up. *Thanks for checking on me ;)*

Her heart stalled when the little *Read* receipt flashed beneath her message, but Gretchen forced herself to refocus on the paragraph about materials.

It was no use. Three cycling dots hooked her attention on her screen, and anticipation over what Theo would say pulled her breath out in fast rhythm. Which was stupid. Theo annoyed her, mostly.

The front door slammed shut, startling Gretchen away from her conflict of heart.

Ky and Dakota never slammed the door. It was a good day when they so much as *closed* the door after themselves, actually.

"Mom?" Gretchen hollered loudly.

No answer.

Curious and filled with trepidation, she tossed the book to the foot of her bed, scooped up her phone, and left her room.

Dropping down the stairs one by one, Gretchen scanned the foyer and parlor for signs of an intruder. She gripped her phone more tightly and considered tapping 9-1-1 into it, just in case.

But as she landed on the first floor and turned toward the kitchen, her mother appeared—alone—, hunched over the table, her body heaving in sobs.

Chapter 4 — Maggie

"**D**id you see this?" Maggie held up the pink page she'd torn from the front door moments earlier. Each corner had been ripped apart, and now four, triangular pieces of tape were left behind on the wood, leaving in the shadow of the doomed document nothing more than a hollow frame.

Gretchen shook her head slowly, "No... well, yeah, but no. I didn't—"

Maggie rubbed the back of her hand across her face, smearing her makeup, and then sank down into the chair Becky had occupied only hours earlier. When the world was full of possibilities. When a bright future teased her in the form of a short, white stack of legalese.

Now, it felt like the walls were closing in. Walls of the house she'd built with her family, or in spite of them. Walls of the house she'd one day renovate because it had *so much potential. A great location! A beautiful family home!* Walls of the house that never got its makeover because its owners were still trying to make do.

"What have you been doing?" A stab of guilt followed Maggie's stricken accusation, but Gretchen didn't get smart.

"I was at work. Then I came home. I saw it but my phone rang, and I got distracted. I went upstairs to read, I— why, Mom? What is it?" Fear flooded the girl's face, and Maggie couldn't well condemn her. She was just a child. It wasn't her fault. It wasn't Gretchen's fault that Maggie had no control over the household finances. Or her husband. It wasn't Gretchen's fault that Maggie had tolerated Travis for this long.

"Never mind," she answered, punching numbers into her cell phone.

Gretchen reached for the paper, and Maggie couldn't help but to allow her to read it. Shock absorbed both their faces as Travis's line rang and rang.

"Mom?" Gretchen glanced up from the thin page, staring blankly at Maggie. "Do we have to leave?"

Maggie swallowed hard, and the line continued ringing. "Your dad isn't answering." She hung up and dialed again, looking frantically around the kitchen as if a clue might reveal itself.

A second call was equally fruitless.

"I'll try," Gretchen offered, tears budding along her lower lash line. Maggie nodded and bounded into the parlor, which they'd used as something of an office. Travis kept a couple boxes of paperwork in there, and Maggie always knew to toss her receipts and bills on top of the pile along with his mail. Each year come tax season, he would see to ordering it and hauling it to a professional off Main Street. What was the accountant's name? Maggie's mind had turned to mush as soon as she'd read the words: *Notice of Foreclosure*.

How could she be so stupid to let *Travis* handle their finances?

She knew the answer.

There was no choice. He managed everything from what type of vehicles they could purchase down to what they ate for dinner each night. He decided when Maggie could start doing hair again. He decided she wouldn't rent a space in the lone salon in town, but that instead she could open shop in their kitchen. At the time of his suggestion, the young mother was more than agreeable. After all, an in-home salon sounded as quaint and charming as *Steel Magnolias*.

Then Maggie had remembered how that movie ended, and it changed her opinion. But Travis didn't care. If she wanted to work, she could work in their house. That way, she was always available for him and the children no matter what.

"No answer." Gretchen was standing in the doorway, her phone dangling from one hand.

Maggie pushed up from the messy box of papers. "Briar," she answered, her heart skipping a beat. "I have to pick up Briar. Now."

She raced to her SUV, and Gretchen followed, jumping in and shutting the door.

"Wait," Maggie said. "The boys."

"School bus doesn't arrive for half an hour. We can make it," Gretchen answered urgently, clearly set on joining Maggie to head to Travis's mother's house.

Maggie threw the beast of a vehicle into reverse and peeled out of their garage, through slick, snowy tracks down the long drive and out onto Pine Tree Lane before careening through a four-way stop and speeding up the hill past the high school, where Mrs. Engel had lived since forever.

It was irrational, her fear. But Travis always at least texted. "He *must* know about this," she murmured under her breath. More suppositions filled her head, but she kept them quiet, instead opting to shape a plan. *Get Briar. Get home before the boys. Pack. Get out.* It didn't matter if they had weeks or months to fight the notice. She didn't want to be around in case Travis *did* show back up.

It was her chance. And she was taking it.

"He knows he hasn't been paying the mortgage," Gretchen reasoned beside her.

Maggie shook her head. "*I* should have known he hasn't been paying the mortgage. How could this happen? Gretchen, I'm sorry. I'm sorry." It came out as a whisper beneath a fresh stream of tears. Her daughter's slight hand patted her shoulder just as they pulled up to a stop in front of the Engel home, a stout ranch-style three-bedroom that Maggie herself never thought of as a particularly comfortable place, despite its cozy setting against the base of Hickory Hill.

"Stay here. I'll be back." She left the SUV running and ran up the front walk and to the door, which she slammed her fist against three times before moving her second hand to the doorknob.

It turned in Maggie's palm but the door was already swinging back as her hand remained frozen in place, her mouth agape.

"Hi Mama!" Briar answered the door like she, herself, was the one in charge. All four years of her little life had, ridiculously, flashed in Maggie's mind until just then, and she scooped the sassy child up and hugged her hard.

Mrs. Engel's figure appeared behind them, an apron tied neatly behind her, an even expression on her face. "Hello, Margaret," she said. The older woman's smile didn't reach her eyes. It never did.

Maggie let out a breath while Briar slithered down her body and ran past her to the SUV. "Sissy's here, too?"

The opening and shutting of the vehicle's doors assured Maggie for the moment, as she geared up to ask the question that was burning on her tongue. "Have you heard from Travis today?"

Mrs. Engel shook her head, innocent as any grandmother. "No, why?"

Maggie considered her options but decided to keep her hand close after all. "Just wondering. He was—uh, supposed to call me earlier. Never mind. All's well. Thanks!" She flashed a broad grin, turned, and strode purposefully to the SUV and away from that cold, cold woman for what would hopefully be the last time ever.

Chapter 5 — Rhett

Rhett pressed the heels of his hands into his eye sockets. "What do you mean they *sold* it?"

Zack Durbin lifted his palms in supplication. "I'm sorry, man. Gary Hart bought it through a cash deal."

"Didn't Greta sign something to transfer it to a trust or something?" He was confused and tired. But mostly, crushed. Those acres were all that Rhett had planned for. His way out of his soured relationship with Emma.

Sure, he could still break up with her. And would. He could still find a different house or apartment. He could crash with a buddy until one of his tenants moved out. But Rhett was a stubborn guy. The plan was to build on the land in Hickory Grove. Small town. Fresh start. Different life. Happier life.

Heading back to Louisville would now feel like returning to prison. Rhett's girlfriend wasn't a bad person. But they simply learned, over the last several years, that they had nothing in common. Namely, Emma didn't want children. Ever. For any reason. Rhett wasn't sure himself, but he certainly wanted the *option*. What was worse was that neither could admit how far they'd grown apart. Each had fallen prey to the sunk cost fallacy. Too late to get out.

Rhett fiddled with his phone as Zack shuffled through deeper pages, looking for some trace of hope to offer his former high school buddy.

He came up empty, apparently. "I'm real sorry, Rhett. Maybe you could go to Gary and see about buying it back. He hasn't developed the land yet. There's still a chance you could save it."

Rhett thought about this. It wasn't a bad idea. "Yeah, maybe," he replied, offering half a grin to Zack.

The two shook hands, and Rhett left, dialing the garage on his way out to check on the truck.

No answer.

Typical Travis Engel.

Hickory Grove was small, but trekking up Main Street and down was getting old. He'd like his truck back before making one last ditch effort at recovering what was supposed to be his future.

Maggie's text still sat in his inbox, unanswered and now irrelevant. Initially, he was excited to touch base with the redhead who, decades earlier, came to all his baseball games and cheered him on like a goofball. The girl he sat next to in Biology. The one who giggled during *the talk* and made him raise his hand and ask her question for her. He'd borne the embarrassing task and dealt with the snide laughs from the other guys in the class. Rhett would do it all over again.

Now, as he stared at her words on the screen, he thought back to the moment their friendship solidified. It was before she had agreed to go out with Travis. Before he dated girl after girl, always searching for the one who would live up to his impossible expectations.

It was his sophomore year of high school. Maggie and Rhett had known each other since pre-K, but they'd never had reason to talk much before that day. He was doing yard work around Little Flock Catholic Church—his parents made him, but he didn't mind it so much—when she arrived.

It was a Saturday, just before four o'clock.

Confession.

A woman too old to be Maggie's mom was pulling her by the elbow in tight jerks all the way to the building; the woman's dull heels echoed up the church steps and through the vestry doors.

They'd locked eyes, Maggie and Rhett, but he knew better than to say hello.

Still, the teenaged boy mustered up the guts to check on her the next day. In Geometry.

Through notes passed back and forth all period, he'd learned that Maggie and her brother, Dirk—Rhett's baseball teammate—were raised by their Great Aunt Marguerite. Well, ol' Marguerite discovered that Maggie was wearing lipstick to school. One thing led to another, and the elderly aunt forced her to confession for a litany of other offenses.

The two instant friends carried their conversation to lunch and wound up laughing over Maggie's predicament. But deep down, they both knew it wasn't the happy home Maggie longed for. A home with a mother and father. Not an apartment to which the older woman had condemned the three of them since she had no interest in tending to a garden or mowing grass.

It was a severe existence, and Rhett often wondered if that was why she gravitated toward Travis, whose mother was similarly strict and often mean. Familiarity.

Now, as he stood in front of the Hickory Grove auto shop, he again glanced down at her message. He told himself if the truck wasn't done, then it was a sign, and he had better text her back and accept the invitation for a sweet tea.

Sure enough, as Rhett walked up toward the front doors, he saw the sign: *Closed.* A chill rattled him through his coat as he came to the stark realization that he'd been both bamboozled by a loser and was in a city not his own without any means of transportation.

Maggie's offer now felt awkward. He'd be showing up to her house on foot like some sort of hobo.

No way.

Even heading to Gary Hart's realty office became a fool's task. He could call his sister to drive the two hours down. He could call a cab and pay the exorbitant fee. But no. Rhett wasn't about to let his truck rust in the snow outside of Travis's garage.

Maggie was, actually, the logical choice.

"HEY, STRANGER," RHETT said into the phone line. He squeezed his eyes shut as he pulled his coat more tightly around his torso outside the bank.

"Rhett, um," Maggie began, her voice strained. Background noise overwhelmed their connection. Rhett shifted his phone to the other ear. "Actually, I'm so sorry, something's come up, and I can't talk right now."

He frowned. "Oh? All right, well that's okay but before you go—"

"Really, Rhett. Something's come up. It's sort of serious."

"Maggie, are you okay?"

He thought he heard her sniffle, but children's voices drowned out her voice as she tried for an answer. "Yes, we're fine. I'll call you when I get a chance. Rain check, okay?"

"Wait, Maggie." No matter her circumstances, he had to get his truck back. Travis had the key. "Can I talk to Travis, then?"

"No," she spat.

He started to explain himself, but the line was dead, and Rhett was now entirely out of luck. Could they be in trouble? Running from the law? Was Maggie caught up in some loser scheme with her loser husband?

Rhett hoped not, but it sounded shady. He mulled over his options, finally deciding on heading to Gary Hart's office. At least there he'd be in a warm place to make a decision. And by then, maybe Maggie would be ready to talk.

Chapter 6 — Gretchen

G retchen was packing her suitcase, miserably and weepily. She'd never exactly adored their strange house on Pine Tree Lane.

Her parents had gotten it as a foreclosure. Once the previous owners passed away, their children had allowed the five-bedroom Victorian to fall into relative disrepair until the bank repossessed it. At the time, Gretchen had a vague memory of great hope among the growing Engel brood.

She could picture her mother respectfully asking Great Aunt Marguerite to help her make curtains for the front windows. A recollection of touring a carpet warehouse in Louisville became especially vivid. She could smell the carpet backing and fibers still now, as she carefully folded a pair of jeans and tucked it along the bottom of her roll-on luggage piece.

Presently, uncertainty colored the situation. The notice read final, but there was a phone number and name to contact for further information. Gretchen gathered from listening in on her mother's phone call that the mortgage was underwater by a few months. Sporadic payments had been made previously, already setting in motion a concern on the part of the lenders.

As of now, the bank owned the house, and if the Engels wished to re-establish the mortgage, both parties would need to meet an official on Main Street.

But none of that demanded that they *vacate the premises*, as her mother was demanding they do. Gretchen suspected Maggie was overreacting. Or preparing for something far worse than an eviction.

Did they really have to leave immediately? She'd asked as much, and her mother explained that yes, they had to go. Today. Pack whatever they needed for a few nights and throw it in the SUV.

She'd send someone for the furniture. Who knew? Maybe they *would* come back. But, for now, it was sayonara Pine Tree Lane.

A few hours later, once Dakota and Ky finally got their acts together and Briar had stopped sobbing, and their most prized possessions were loaded haphazardly into frumpy shipping boxes they'd dug from the garage, the four Engels sat. Quiet. Watching light flakes drift down onto the driveway in slow succession.

"Mama, it's cold. At least start the car," Dakota whined from the third row seat.

"Hush up," Maggie snapped. "I'm thinking."

She took in deep breaths, her hands at ten and two on the steering wheel. Her knuckles white.

Gretchen turned to face her siblings. "Listen, you all. Mom is going to figure this out. We just have to be quiet and patient. Even you," she jabbed a tickle at Briar's belly and offered a small smile. "Hey, I know. Let's play the Quiet Game, okay?"

"What's the Quiet Game?" Briar asked through a mouthful of Goldfish crackers.

"Whoever can be quiet the longest gets to watch videos on my phone when we get to where we're going. Deal?"

"Deal!" three voices chimed in at once. The allure of getting to use their big sister's cell phone was enough to distract them from the fact that no one had any idea where they were going.

Gretchen eased back into her seat and studied her mom. Fine lines had grown in around her eyes like spindly branches. Her freckles no longer gave off a sweetness, but instead looked more like age spots. This was all evident despite the smudges from her make up.

"Here, Mom," she pulled two diaper wipes from the spare package on the console and passed them to Maggie, who held out her hand blindly, took the wipes, and rubbed her face up and down in tired, swooping circles.

"Thanks," Maggie whispered, wadding the wet sheets into a ball and stuffing them inside an empty cup holder. She sucked in a deep breath and blew it out before turning her head to Gretchen. "I have an idea."

THEY PULLED UP TO HICKORY Grove Realty. Gretchen turned in her seat and declared Dakota the winner of the Quiet Game. Ky and Briar moaned, but Dakota, in true middle-child fashion, agreed to share. It would have been a departure for most adolescent boys, but Dakota and Ky were mature. Even keeled and easy going. Which was helping right about then.

"One sec, though," Gretchen warned, as her mother un-buckled her seatbelt and told the kids to sit tight. Gretchen desperately wanted to join her mom. Her need for information was dire, but being eighteen didn't deprive her of her duty to be a big sister first.

Before she passed back the device, she tapped out a message to Theo. She needed to confide in someone she could trust. And Theo might be able to help. If he couldn't, his mom sure would.

"Okay," Gretchen said at last, hitting send and passing the phone back to Dakota who took it and thanked her.

Having nothing else to do, Gretchen simply sat and prayed. She prayed Mr. Gary would have a rental. She prayed her mom's credit wasn't affected. She prayed hardest, though, that her dad was slimy enough to leave town for good and never look back.

Because, really, if Gretchen and her siblings could shake free of the controlling jerk of a father, then they could do with-out a big house on a nice street. Especially one that never did get that pretty new carpet.

Chapter 7 — Maggie

Maggie knew she could call Becky. Or maybe even Fern. But her pride was bigger than that. And, anyway, if she could solve this thing right now—if she could find a great little rental and sign her name on the dotted line—then everything would be just fine. No need to drag her kids into someone else's house. No need to dive into the details of her dysfunctional world.

Gary Hart leaned forward and propped his elbows on the desk in front of him. The shift of his heft pushed air out from the cushion of his chair, and he winced in embarrassment. But he pushed ahead, undaunted. "Your credit's shot to heck, Hun," he answered. The flesh of his elbows rubbed across the varnished finish, and Maggie wondered why on earth he was wearing short sleeves in such weather.

The man dabbed at a sheet of sweat forming along his hairline, which was high enough to nearly disappear from sight. She closed her eyes and forced herself to be nice. And patient. And hopeful. She had no room to judge this kind man. No room at all. "I think I can get cash, Mr. Hart." *Why hadn't she stopped at the bank first?*

"You can't sign a lease agreement without even marginal credit, Hun. I'm terribly sorry. You know, I have a sister who might rent to you. Up in Corydon..."

Maggie shook her head. "I can't move. It has to be local. My kids are in school here. My clients are here. You don't know of anyone who'd be willing to... *work* with me?"

Gary Hart's expression softened. "Listen, Miss Maggie. I'll make some calls. You know property management is not my main line of business here. Leave me your phone number, and I'll be in touch if I can find anything. All right, Hun?"

She nodded and took his business card, flipping it over to jot down her number before thanking him and rising.

With no family to impose on, and no friends she was willing to humiliate herself in front of, Maggie stomped out to the SUV.

"Well?" Gretchen pressed as soon as the door fell closed.

"He'll call us if something comes up." Maggie put the car in reverse and briefly checked over her shoulder just in time to avoid backing squarely into a clearly confused man wandering through the parking lot. "Crud knuckles!" Maggie sputtered, darting a glance in her rearview to see the boys focused on a screen and Briar babbling to her doll. Maggie's heartbeat shot to triple pace and fell back again.

Gretchen twisted in her seat. "Hey, I know him," she said, her voice a murmur.

Initially inclined to wait a second then speed off and up the hill toward Hickory Grove Inn, Maggie glanced at her daughter who repeated herself. "Mom, I know that man."

Exasperated, Maggie asked her how she knew him then squinted into her side view mirror to get a better look. "Oh my Lord, it's *Rhett Houston*." Immediately, she slunk deep down in her seat and waved at Gretchen to do the same. "How the heck do *you* know *him?"* she hissed to her daughter as she kept her face firmly turned from the window.

A giggle escaped the teenager's mouth. "He came into Mally's today. Ordered a burger and coffee and chatted with Theo. Said he knew *you*," Gretchen concluded pointedly.

A flush crept up Maggie's neck as she peeked over the door to discover the coast was clear. "Yes, well," she answered, straightening and backing out carefully so as not to draw attention. "We were friends in high school. That's all. Wonder why he's walking around Hickory Grove?"

"Theo said he blew a tire on the way here. He's moving back home, he told us. Has land somewhere. Gonna build on it." Gretchen was growing bored of the conversation, and Maggie had no energy to devote to someone she barely knew anymore.

"Mama, where are we going? I'm hungry," Ky called from the far back seat.

Maggie shifted into gear and took off. "We're going to stay in a hotel everyone," she declared, smiling as genuine a smile as she could muster. "And you can even order room service!"

Gretchen flicked a sidelong glance to her mother. "Since when does the Hickory Grove Inn offer *room service?"*

Just as Maggie began to shoot a smart retort to her oldest, Dakota interrupted. "Gretch, you're getting a phone call."

"Who is it?" Gretchen asked.

"Miss Becky."

"Oh, shoot," Gretchen replied. "Just let it go to voicemail."

Dakota took the direction, and then Maggie's own phone buzzed to life on the console. Now entirely suspicious, she took a deep breath. "I take it you told Becky. Answer my phone, Gretchen May Engel."

Gretchen snatched up the device and held it to her chest. "I'm sorry, Mom. I told *Theo*. I wanted to help."

"You told him about our business? Becky Linden is *my* best friend. She already knows my business. If I want to tell her more of it, then I reserve that right from now on. Give me the dang phone, young lady."

The eighteen-year-old tapped *Accept* and passed the device over.

"Hi, Beck." Maggie sighed into the phone before launching into a full-blown explanation of the day's events.

Yes, everyone's fine.

No, they didn't need her help.

She promised. She swore.

No, they couldn't stay in the house. Not even one more night.

Technically, yes, they could stay in the house several more nights, but it was a true eviction notice.

Bank-owned.

Maggie had to leave. With the kids. Pronto.

Becky pressed her on this one. "Is it Travis? Are you afraid of him?"

Maggie glanced to Gretchen who was watching and listening as well as she could through the squabbling in the back seat.

"No," Maggie replied. "But I don't think it's smart for us to sit there and wait. The woman on the phone said an offer had been made on the house, and if I can't match or beat it with cash, then the new owners could make us leave immediately."

Becky fought this point, claiming she could bring Zack Durbin in on the case, but Maggie refused. She did not have the cash. And if Travis did, then maybe pigs could fly, too. And even if pigs could fly, Maggie saw the whole mess as her chance to get out from under him. "I'll figure something out," Maggie insisted. "I don't want to discuss it right now. Kids are here." She looked over her shoulder.

"Maggie, what is your long-term plan? You can't just live in a hotel room indefinitely."

Her best friend had a point. "True. Okay, Beck. If I can't pull something together in two nights, then I'll ask Zack for help. Deal?"

"Deal," Becky huffed. "Mags, just... be *smart* for once, okay?"

It took every last ounce of strength Maggie could muster not to totally hang up on her friend. Pulling from her deepest reserves, she bid Becky a terse farewell just as they pulled up to the Hickory Grove Inn.

The building itself was a converted mansion or boarding house of some sort. Practically ancient—for the area—and looming at the very end of Overlook Lane. But the new owner had made it work as a cross between a hostel and a charming bed-and-breakfast.

Maggie left the children in the car to go and see about a vacancy. The snow had finally stopped, and she moved quickly up the crumbly, salted steps wondering what in the world she would do if there were no available rooms.

Her phone buzzed in her pocket, and she stalled outside the front door to answer it. *Fern Gale.*

Great.

"Hi, Fern," Maggie answered, unwilling to avoid the inevitable. "I guess you heard? Or saw?" Though Fern was Maggie's next-door neighbor, that didn't mean she had instant access to the drama unfolding one door down. On Pine Tree Lane, every property was over an acre in size, and Fern's was several.

Fern's warm voice nearly brought Maggie to tears. Any pity was hard to take, but coming from sweet Fern—the redhead almost broke. "Maggie, I hope you will bring the kids here to stay. You know I have more than enough room. I'd love to have you."

Maggie thanked her second-best friend profusely but declined, asserting that they had a plan and all would be well. She swallowed a sob.

"What about all your belongings?" Fern pried.

"I'll get them. I just—I need space. I'll send someone. Hire someone, even. We wanted to make a clean break." Maggie cringed at her own turn of phrase. She wasn't running from anything.

Was she?

Chapter 8 — Rhett

R hett was tired of treading slippery sidewalks and through the snow-encrusted intersections of downtown Hickory Grove, so he took Gary Hart up on his offer of a ride.

It was a pity offer. The realtor had sworn up and down that if he knew Rhett was coming back to Hickory Grove, he never would have signed the contract to build a storefront on the Houston's former land.

But the money had already changed hands. The plans were set. Rhett could have offered double what Gary had paid, but he knew—deep down—that it wasn't meant to be.

Rhett hadn't been much of a religious man in his adulthood, but he believed that when God closed a door, he opened a window. *Somewhere*.

However, outbidding the pot-bellied realtor was not an open window.

"Got a place in mind? The garage?" Gary asked as the car engine's hum reached their seats.

Rhett sat quietly, his phone uselessly cupped in his hand, and considered his options. The garage was closed, obviously. He could kill more time at Mally's until someone came to pick him up, but who would?

The last thing he wanted to do was to call Emma. He didn't want to deal with her passive aggressive comments and questions, like why he hadn't replaced his spare tire a year before. He didn't want to deal with her subtle irritation at having to drive over an hour-and-a-half on a Monday night.

She had work the next morning, Rhett. He could hear her now. And it was true. No one wanted to take their evening to drive into Indiana and back. It was a rough spot to be sure.

And, anyway, he still had to get his truck back. There was no point in going anywhere... not yet.

"Any motels crop up in town lately?" he asked Gary. "I'm sure Travis will be back tomorrow. I can get my truck then and get outta Dodge." What he didn't add was that the whole experience had cemented in him the deep aversion to *ever* returning to Hickory Grove.

"Sounds good. I know a place," Gary answered, nodding along as he rolled out of his office and onto Main Street. "And Rhett, if you decide you do want to make a home here, I know a place that might come open in the near future."

"Oh?" Rhett replied, humoring the older man.

"Sure, sure. Pine Tree Lane. The Engel house. They went underwater months ago. The bank is finally putting their foot down with those folks. Now, someone else recently made an offer, mind you, but if it falls through—"

Gary kept jabbering away, but Rhett had stopped listening. Pressure built in his ears and a pain cut through his heart. "Hang on. Are you talking about *Maggie Devereux's* house?"

The realtor bristled, his ruddy cheeks turning a deeper shade of red and his smile dropping into a deep frown. "Why, yes. It's a sad, sad situation. I admit. She was in my office just before you showed up, in fact. Trying to bribe me, I might add." The round man huffed, but Rhett couldn't refrain from an eye roll. "Now, don't get me wrong, Rhett. I like Maggie and her friend Becky just fine. Really, I do. They are lovely ladies. But it's not my fault she—"

"—Married a loser?" Rhett finished the man's sentence in time for the sedan to heave to a stop outside their destination. "Thanks for the ride, Gary." He popped out of the car and let the door fall shut without so much as a wave.

Shoving his hands in his coat pocket, Rhett stomped up and away from the steaming vehicle. He knew Gary was a good person at heart. But his gossip was unwelcome. Especially when it came to two dear friends, one of whom needed help rather than judgment. It occurred to Rhett, as he opened the front door to a clanging bell above, exactly why Maggie had hung up on him.

She was in a crisis.

A far deeper crisis than Rhett. But what also dawned on him was that he may not get his tire fixed anytime soon. And Travis Engel may not be the one to do it at all.

For all he knew, Travis and Maggie and Gretchen and the rest of the Engel clan had already bailed out of town.

It made perfect and crushing sense. Maybe there was no use in getting a room for the night, after all.

Desperate and disappointed, he reluctantly tapped a quick text to Emma, bringing her up to speed and telling her he would need his spare truck key and a spare tire or else he'd have to have the beast towed back to Louisville, which felt somehow crummier than his original idea of sticking around.

Unsurprisingly, her reply came immediately. Though she hadn't said no, the tone of her message was clear. If Rhett expected Emma to drive into Hickory Grove and back to

Louisville all on a Monday night, then he'd be wishing he'd just paid for a room and prayed Travis was still around somewhere.

Rhett blew out a sigh and replied that he'd figure it out, no thanks to her, before slipping the phone back in his pocket and opening the door to the Hickory Grove Inn.

Chapter 9 — Maggie

The clerk had just handed Maggie two room keys—newfangled key cards were still a thing of the future in tiny Hickory Grove—complete with weathered plastic keychain tags, when she turned around and stepped smack into the solid torso of a towering man. "Sorry," she muttered, her eyes downcast as she tried to circumnavigate his imposing shape in order to return to the kids.

The worrisome redhead nibbled at flakes of dry skin around her thumbnail as she thought ahead to digging through Travis's boxes of financial records in the hopes of finding a clue. Something that would help her piece together her plan. Her neck had grown achy with tension and a headache nagged along her temples.

"*Maggie?*" An incredulous—and familiar—voice snapped her to attention.

Her hand dropped to her side and she gawked up. "*Rhett?*" She couldn't help it. A broad smile broke out across her face. Maggie shook her head. "*Rhett Houston?*" she repeated, remembering his text and phone call from earlier in the day. It felt like a whole week had passed since she hung up on him.

He opened his hands in surprise, and in spite of herself, she copied the gesture, and—awkwardly—they fell into a warm hug. It reminded her of high school. He even smelled the same.

"Are you still wearing Curve?" she accused playfully, though on the inside a groan crept up. The last thing she wanted was to explain to her old friend why she was holing up in a local B&B for the night.

A white lie tickled its way to her head.

Rhett chuckled and nodded, releasing her as his face fell. "So," he began awkwardly, his face creased in either sympathy or confusion. She couldn't quite read it.

"Oh, you're probably wondering what we're doing here." A high-pitched laugh fumbled its way out of her mouth.

He studied her, his brows falling low over his eyes. "Well, I—"

"A pipe burst. Water leak. The whole kitchen is flooded, and the water isn't stopping anytime soon..."

"Oh," he answered, scratching his jaw and averting his gaze beyond her to the clerk, and Maggie knew that Rhett knew exactly when she was fibbing and when she was telling the truth. He did back in twelfth grade and he did right in that moment. She tried her best to hold her ground, but he cleared his throat meaningfully. "I'm very sorry to hear that. Must be hard. Where's your, ah... Where's, um..."

"Travis?" His name tasted like sour milk on her tongue. "Gone, I hope." Maggie caught herself. "Well, I don't know. It's complicated. Um," she shook her head and pressed her fingers to her forehead. "Sorry, Rhett. Like I said, it's been a long day, and—"

"Let's grab a drink. You can tell me about it," he answered, his consternation turning to warmth.

Maggie sighed deeply. A drink with Rhett Houston would probably solve every single one of her problems. "The kids," she replied, lifting her hand helplessly toward the car. "I have to get them inside."

He nodded. "After?"

A smile softened the lines across her forehead. "That would be great, really. But it's not a good time."

"Maggie," he whispered. "Can I help?"

She stared up at him, tears welling behind her eyes. Swallowing, she replied, "I wish you could."

ONCE MAGGIE HAD LEFT Rhett to check himself in, she all but jogged out to the SUV, waving to the kids frantically that they could get out. Gretchen unbuckled Briar, and the boys rounded to the back of the SUV and grabbed their overnight bags.

"Mama, do we need to bring these boxes?" Dakota asked, his expression serious.

She scruffed his hair and answered that yes, but she'd bring them in.

"Why? It's not like we're staying here." Gretchen pointed out as Briar grew drowsy on her hip.

"I need to go through Travis's paperwork. See what I missed. Maybe we have recourse."

"Why can't we just sleep in our own house, Mama?" Ky asked innocently.

"I told you all: we're going to have a little vacation. I'm not quite sure what happened with the house, and—" She hesitated, feeling four sets of eyes on her, expectant.

Dakota blew out a sigh. A little boy on the verge of becoming a man. "Where's Dad?"

"That's the other thing," Maggie confessed. "I need to get ahold of him. But you three have nothing to worry about, okay? I'll fix this." Her eyes bubbled with tears, and Gretchen caught the emotion, her face stretching into an ugly cry.

Chapter 10 — Gretchen

"**M**aybe we should squeeze into one room together," Gretchen suggested, as they stood together in front of their first room at the end of the second-floor hall. "You know, save money while we can?"

Their mother shook her head. At the bank en route to the Inn, Maggie had pulled all but one hundred dollars from their checking account and the same from their savings. Gretchen had asked if it would be enough, to which Maggie had replied that they were set. For weeks, if not a month or more.

But to her mother's credit, there *were* five of them and each room had only a double bed. No sofa or pull-out. Such were the options for a last-minute booking in the charming little bed-and-breakfast.

"We can't fit in one room. We'll hardly fit in two. I'll stay with the boys and sleep on the ground if I have to. You and Briar will share that room." Maggie lifted her chin toward the door at the far end of the hall. "Get settled, then bring Briar over, and we'll make supper plans."

NOT FIVE MINUTES LATER, Gretchen dragged a tantrum-throwing Briar over to the room next door. Inside, her mother was elbow deep into a crowded heap of unopened mail and coffee-stained pages. Gretchen let down the kicking and screaming child and took in the even-smaller room. "I thought you had a double bed?" she asked Ky who lay stretched across a most-decidedly twin-sized bed with his nose in a comic book and both shoes dangling precariously from his toes. "And aren't we getting dinner? Why aren't you all ready?"

Briar, wailing and clinging passionately to her ragged blankie, tore across the room, tackling Maggie.

"Briar, stop this fussing," their mother hushed the little girl, tucking her under one arm as she continued to claw through papers.

"Mom? What about dinner? We're hungry. *Clearly*," Gretchen muttered the last word, her eyes narrowing on Briar whose sobs turned to sniffles as she snuggled against Maggie's shoulder.

"All right," Maggie responded, pushing herself up off the ground with Briar still crooked in her arm. "You're right. Let's order a pizza."

Cheers took the place of the group's irritation, and even Gretchen was pleased with the suggestion. She pulled up a search on her phone and tapped squarely on Pappy's Pizzeria. "Delivery or take-out?" she hissed across to her mother.

"We could go there?"

"No," wailed Ky. "I don't want to get back in the car."

"Delivery," Maggie agreed, bouncing Briar up and down.

After a quick order, Gretchen clicked her phone off and strode to the mess of paperwork. "What are you looking for?" she asked her mother, whose attention was now focused on finding a cartoon for the boys.

"Anything," the bedraggled woman replied, settling on a nature show for Briar's benefit.

"Come on, Mama. We don't want to watch this," Dakota whined. "Besides, Briar always gets to pick at home."

The little girl wasn't watching anyway. Instead, she had climbed down from her mother's side and plopped herself right next to the box before tossing her treasured blanket and digging right into the stack.

"Briar, no," Maggie snapped.

Gretchen took stock of the situation and spoke up. "Mom, here, let me take Briar out. We can tour the gift shop. You keep searching, and the boys can watch their show."

Maggie nodded gratefully.

"And Mom," Gretchen added, as she reached for Briar's hand. "Let's swap rooms. You three take the double bed. Bri and I can squeeze in here easily." Her eyes swept the room, and a sense of pity fell over her. They couldn't stay at the Inn for very long. They needed an out and fast.

Gretchen walked Briar down the hardwood staircase and into the lobby, wondering why her mother wouldn't allow them to stay with Miss Becky, when she remembered just how powerful her mother's sense of pride could be.

She didn't realize it until the boys begged to sleep over at their friends' houses and Maggie told them, "*In this family, we don't invite ourselves to stay with other people.*"

But they *had* an invitation. With Miss Becky *and* with Miss Fern.

More than her feelings of desperation, a rage began to churn inside Gretchen. Rage over her father's uselessness. Rage over a lifetime of him controlling their every move only to vanish into thin air.

Both Maggie and Gretchen had tried calling him a dozen more times to no avail. They were stuck, and it felt miserable.

Gretchen prodded Briar into the modest gift shop as she pulled her phone from her pocket and tried something else. A different number.

It rang only once. As always.

"Engel residence," came the terse greeting.

"Mamaw Engel?" Gretchen spoke low.

"Yes? Who's calling?"

As though the woman had dozens of grandchildren.

"It's Gretchen, Mamaw."

A pause. And then, "Hello, Gretchen. Is everything all right?"

"No, actually. We—" she stopped in the middle of her sentence as her eyes took hold of a familiar figure entering through the front doors.

"What's the matter, Gretchen?" The woman's cold voice was neither reassuring nor helpful, and Gretchen realized, in that moment, why Maggie hadn't called her mother-in-law. Why she refused to seek refuge there or maybe anywhere.

It was an *adult* moment. For Gretchen. A moment when the presence of a veritable stranger suddenly felt more comforting than the voice of her own grandmother.

Without another word, in honor of her mother's pride and in hopes that the answer lay just before her eyes, Gretchen simply hung up the phone.

The eighteen-year-old scooped Briar into her arms and turned on her heel in time to face the gentleman who, with as lost an expression on his face as ever, was inquiring about toothpaste and a toothbrush, among other toiletries.

Gretchen stepped up behind him, tapped him on the shoulder, and with the boldness of a girl with a plan, threw her shoulders back as well as she could with a preschooler on her hip.

At last, she cleared her voice in time for him to turn around and frown down at her. Unfaltering, Gretchen spoke. "Mr. Houston?"

Chapter 11 — Rhett

"Are you getting a room here? Can my mom stay with you for the night? We're cramped as can be."

Rhett thanked the hotelier for the toiletries and smirked at the young woman standing proudly before him. A little freckle-faced child clung to the familiar girl for dear life as they awaited his response.

"Gretchen, right?" he asked, smiling to hide his confusion.

"That's right, Mr. Houston. We met at the diner. Sorry for being... rude earlier. It's been a weird day. Anyway, I guess you're staying here, too?"

He wasn't sure where to take the conversation with this changed teenager. Her fast progression from bubblegum-snapping-waitress-with-an-attitude to desperate big sister was a lot to take in.

And anyway, Maggie had declined his invitation of a drink—understandably. But to share his room with her?

"Why?" he asked earnestly, gesturing they seek a more private corner of the foyer.

Gretchen followed until they were in the kitchen, which was open to guests, apparently. The Hickory Grove Inn wasn't around when Rhett was a kid. Well, it *was* around, but it wasn't a bed-and-breakfast back then. It was just short of a haunted mansion, really.

He liked it. Character flowed freely through the un-reno-vated front hall. Heavy furniture and drapery that might have boasted years of dust now shone with polish. The chair rail and sconces all suggested a charm that was missing from the modern age.

Even in the kitchen, quaintness wasn't sacrificed for utility, what with the potbellied cast iron stove beneath which rested a matching antique stove. Rhett felt the pull of the 1700s here in the middle of America. The heartland.

Maggie's daughter blew a strand of hair from her eyes and shifted the little girl's weight on her hip. The latter whined before burying her strawberry-blonde head into Gretchen's shoulder.

"We have two rooms, but it's too crowded. My room only has a twin bed, actually, and since you know each other—"

"Whoa, whoa, whoa," Rhett held his hands up and backed into a butcher-block kitchen island. "Gretchen, I *knew* your mom. I mean, yes, I *know* her, but we haven't talked much lately. I just saw her earlier, and she seemed a little too preoccupied for a reunion." *Especially an intimate one.*

He considered asking about the water leak but thought better of it. The teenager's face was already twisting into panic.

"Mr. Houston, I thought you were like best friends? 'Rhett Houston.'" She flashed air quotes in gentle sarcasm. "Yeah, my mom and Becky talk about you all the time."

The point was a bullet to his gut, though he didn't quite know why. He scratched his neck then fiddled with the package of his overnight essentials.

"Say, listen. What about your dad? I mean—Travis, right? Is he out of town, or—?" Rhett was asking more for the benefit of figuring out what to do about his truck rather than whether it would even be appropriate to so much as take a step inside Maggie's guest room.

"He's a—" Her reply came with force but she stopped just as feverishly, glancing down at her sister and blinking. "He's not here. And we aren't expecting him to show up."

The little one writhed in Gretchen's arms and pointed wildly toward the front door. "Pizza! Sissy, Pizza!"

Rhett's stomach lurched in hunger despite his big lunch—he was *always* hungry.

Gretchen allowed the girl to plop down on her own two feet, and they both began to head toward the teenaged delivery boy who stood askance in the front hall. "Come on, Mr. Rhett. You can carry it up."

And just like that, Rhett Houston was home.

Chapter 12 — Maggie

"Um." It was all she could muster at the sight of the three of them and two large pizzas dwarfed by Rhett's towering frame. "Hi?"

"Mom, we found him checking in. He doesn't even have an overnight bag. Wasn't expecting to stay in town, but guess what?"

"What?" Maggie answered, eyeballing him as she grabbed Briar's hand and awkwardly ushered them into the room. The only thing that comforted her was that Rhett seemed equally uncomfortable.

Gretchen wasn't usually a bubbly girl, and her rambling revealed that her nerves were on fire. Much like Maggie's.

"Mom, he dropped his truck at the garage and *Daddy* never took it in to work on. In fact, Daddy *closed* the shop earlier today." Gretchen laced her slender arms across her chest and threw her weight back onto one hip. "And, I have an idea."

"No, no," Rhett inserted, passing the pizzas over to Maggie. "I'm sorry Gretchen, but that won't work."

"What?" Maggie asked, curious.

"Mom, you can stay with Mr. Rhett to give us more space. At least for tonight. It would make this situation a little more comfortable." Gretchen waved her hand behind her at the boys, squeezed together on what was beginning to look less like a twin bed and more like a narrow shelf with a mattress on top.

"We have a second room, Gretchen," Maggie answered, laughing as lightly as she could. "We're fine." Turning to face Rhett, she said, "I'm so sorry. Gretchen is just trying to help. But really, we're fine. Two rooms are more than enough. Briar is tiny, and—"

"You're welcome to stay with me," he replied, meeting her gaze.

Maggie felt a lump form in her throat. She thought of her husband. She thought of her children. She thought back to high school and the moments she and Rhett shared during passing periods and inside of a class hour.

The glances.

The warmth.

The friendship.

"Well," Maggie began. Ky and Dakota hadn't even reached for a piece of pizza yet. They were staring hard at Rhett. Too hard. "No," she went on, "but thank you. It's a nice offer. And, it was a nice idea, Gretch. But we'll be just fine."

Ky and Dakota relaxed. Gretchen shrugged her shoulders, her mouth setting in a line. Briar was about to pull a whole box of pizza off the edge of the bed.

Rhett, for his part, smiled kindly. "You'd think they'd have more than a twin bed and a television set in here," he commented, glancing over his shoulder at the door. "I'd better go make sure they didn't give me the broom closet..."

Laughter erupted from Maggie, and the children gawked in surprise. She couldn't help it. A full-blown belly laugh overtook her, racking her body until tears—both happy and sad—spilled from her eyes in rapid succession.

A couple faint chuckles cut through her bizarre outbreak, and Rhett spoke up.

"Tell you what, everyone, why don't I take your mom to help me see about my own lodgings while you all dig into the pizza. Sound good?"

Maggie smiled gratefully and told the children she was going to go with Mr. Rhett and would be back in a bit.

Just before she left the room, Dakota hollered out behind her. "Mama, who *is* that guy?"

Gretchen replied before Maggie could even open her mouth. "One of Mom's old friends. He's cool, okay?"

RHETT'S ROOM WAS IDENTICAL to the one initially assigned to her and the boys.

A pretty twin bed protruded from a narrow wall. An old-fashioned tube TV sat soberly on an antique dresser in the corner. One chair—wooden—posed on the far side of the bed, facing into the room, away from the window.

Maggie strode over and stood, pulling the lace curtain back and staring out. The Inn had a view down toward the Little Flock Cemetery. The one where her mother was buried.

She wondered, as she often did, if her father was still alive. Who he was. Where he went.

"I guess it was fate," Maggie snorted, turning to watch Rhett set a few things on the pedestal sink. A plastic toothbrush in its packaging. A white, mini tube of paste.

"What was fate? Us bumping into each other? I'd say Hickory Grove is small enough that it didn't even matter that I was trying to get ahold of you. We still wound up at the same place." He shot her a knowing look, and something welled deep inside Maggie. He seemed... *different*.

In high school, Maggie would have laughed at Rhett's attempts to change the conversation. She'd welcome them. Thankful he *knew* her. He *understood* her. He could take her mind off anything and piece it back together happily elsewhere.

And the next day, she'd beeline straight back into Travis's scrawny teenager arms, running her hand up his sleeve, laying claim to what—at the time—was the hottest ticket in town.

At seventeen-years-old, Travis Engel was the first student at Hickory Grove High School to get a tattoo. Maggie helped him tend to it, since his mother was utterly opposed to the idea.

It was the Engel family crest (something tribal and exotic, which never quite made sense since Engel was an Anglo-Saxon surname) along with Travis's father's initials and birthdate. Like Maggie, Travis had never known his own father. He'd left town before Travis was ever born. Though neither one knew their dads, the differences between the two fatherless teenagers were many. Especially the circumstances of their fathers' absences. Or so she'd always assumed.

Maggie's mother had never made one mention of the man who'd sired her twins. She didn't take his name, and she kept the secret close to her chest. Of course, the twins never got a chance to nag her for details. And Marguerite refused to discuss the subject.

Travis's mother wept over the man who had left her pregnant and took off, burning out of Hickory Grove like a hunted deer.

Rhett knew all this. He'd known it since high school. And so when Maggie asked about her destiny, he knew quite well what she meant.

"Rhett," she answered, sighing deeply. "Why did I marry him?"

"He was... dangerous," Rhett answered, passing her at the window to ease into the chair behind. "Everyone thought so. He had that huge truck. And that scaredy-cat mother. And dumb tattoo. No one told him no. Not even *you*."

She turned and sat neatly on the bed, facing Rhett. "I guess not. I guess I never had to, anyway."

Silence took the place of small talk until Maggie couldn't bear it anymore. She felt Rhett's gaze on her, and looked up to meet it. Fine lines crowded around his pale green eyes. His sandy-colored hair had darkened a little, but he still kept a neat crew cut. And, notably, he still took care of his body. She wondered if his high school football days had turned into intramural evenings at Louisville Community College.

Maggie wrapped an arm around her mom-ish, middle-aged midsection. "I'm so happy to see you, Rhett. I'm sorry I hung up earlier, but I guess you can see what a mess I'm in."

"Maggie," Rhett answered plainly. "What happened with the house?"

Again, she sighed, rubbing the back of her neck and rolling her head around in a stretch. "Ugh. I don't know. I need to find out. Travis did all the bills. He handled everything. I guess he wasn't paying the mortgage, and I never knew about it. I know we paid it a couple months ago though, because I was at the bank for *something*... signing *something*, and it came up. But, I guess—well the lady on the phone told me we've missed six payments. She said the bank had already looked to sell. I don't know how they could do that. But the notice was only for a foreclosure. It's all so confusing, and I am so out of touch with everything. I don't know where to begin." Her face fell into her hands and she hunched over her knees.

Rhett stood and moved to her, bending down to wrap her in a hug. "I'm so sorry," he whispered.

Maggie stood and hugged him back—hard. "I'm stupid," she whispered back.

"You're not stupid. You were... caught up," he answered, joining her on the bed.

"Look at what I've done to my family," she gestured around herself. "My kids. Staying in a *motel*?"

"Hey, now. It's a *bed-and-breakfast*. I'm staying here, too, you know," he joked. She didn't laugh. "Maggie, if this is the worst that happens in your life, you're going to be fine. I can help. Let me, please. I don't have much going on. You can stay in one of my rentals in the city."

She shook her head. "We can't leave Hickory Grove. Thank you, but the kids go to school here. My clients are here. My *life* is here."

"What are you going to do if he comes back? *When* he comes back?"

Maggie bit down on her lower lip. "I'm not afraid of Travis. He would never hurt us, Rhett." Her eyebrows fell together in a deep frown. "And he *is* their father."

Suddenly, Rhett stood. "Listen, I don't want to get in the middle. I didn't realize. I'm sorry."

"No," Maggie answered, panicked. "No, *I'm* sorry. I'm being ridiculous. It's over between Travis and me. That's clear. I just have to figure out what happens next."

The divorce paperwork popped into her mind, and now she wondered just how in the heck she'd ever get a divorce from someone on the lam. Her stomach growled, and her head throbbed.

"You can't stay *here* for long. At least consider finding another place. Or fighting the bank. Maybe you can stay in your house after all?"

Maggie shook her head. "I don't want to be there. I mean, I'm not *afraid* of Travis, but what if he comes back? I can't face him. I don't know what *I* would do. I guess I'm—"

"Afraid of yourself?"

It was a heavy suggestion. And it wasn't all of the truth. But Maggie supposed little had really changed in all those years since Rhett had been gone.

He still *knew* her.

"THERE YOU ARE." GRETCHEN was storming down the hallway just as her mother and Rhett appeared from his room at the opposite end of the hall.

"Is everything okay, Gretch?" Maggie asked, her stomach lurching. They didn't need one more thing to worry about.

Maggie felt Rhett hang back by half a stride.

"Gretchen, what is it?" Maggie pressed. Her oldest daughter's expression wasn't one of panic, but a certain alarm colored the girl's cheeks.

The teenager replied simply, "Mom, I found something."

Chapter 13 — Gretchen

Everyone had crammed into the pizza room. Their mom stood next to the bed near Gretchen, who held the papers taut in her hands.

She continued reading. "... on *behalf of the executor or executors of the estate of Marguerite Lorna Devereux*," Gretchen went on until her mother held up her hand.

"Let me see it," Maggie demanded, urgent. Even Ky, Dakota, and Briar were rapt with attention. An important document was one thing.

A surprise letter in the mail about their recently departed—albeit cranky and even a little scary—aunt was quite another.

Maggie's eyes flashed up at Gretchen. "This was just lying in the stack of pages?"

Mr. Rhett cleared his voice behind them. "I should go..."

"No, it's fine. Maybe you can help me understand it," Gretchen's mother darted a glance to him, but he stayed firmly in his position near the door, hands shoved into pockets.

"Gretchen, was this just sitting in the pile?" Maggie asked again.

"Yeah. Kind of. Well, it was in an envelope. Addressed to you."

"Was the envelope open?"

Gretchen blushed slightly. "Well, no, it was sealed. No one had opened it. Sorry, Mom, but—"

Maggie held up her hand, "No, no. That's totally fine. But I don't understand. It was just sitting there, *unopened*?"

"Lots of mail is sitting in here. I found electric bills. A membership termination notice for the gym."

Gretchen studied her mother. Her neck was growing splotchy and red. She slowly let herself down onto the bed, the letter in hand. "Travis opens the mail. It's what he does every night. He brings the mail in and says he's going to handle bills. Every night." Maggie's eyes tore from the page and searched her children, all who were nodding.

"Obviously Daddy hasn't been telling the truth," Dakota pointed out, innocently.

Ky piped up. "Daddy's no liar."

Maggie held up her hands, effectively shushing the bunch before a quarrel broke out. "Daddy has not been doing a lot of things, but that doesn't matter now. Let's figure this out, all right you all?"

Collective nodding commenced, and Gretchen moved to the bed to read over her mother's shoulder.

Moments passed, and Maggie looked up at Gretchen. "Dirk," her mother said breathlessly.

"What?"

"Dirk. Uncle Dirk. Great Aunt Marguerite named Uncle Dirk the executor. I remember. But nothing ever happened. I didn't think she had anything to leave behind."

Dakota spoke up. "Is that Aunt Lorna?"

Mr. Rhett scratched his jaw at the door. "Lorna?"

Maggie shook her head. "She developed dementia a couple years ago and told everyone her name was Lorna. For sanity's sake, we took her word for it."

"Does the paperwork say Lorna or Marguerite?" Dakota asked.

"Marguerite Lorna," Maggie replied. "I don't think I knew that Lorna was her middle name. Maybe she did go by Lorna as a girl."

It made sense. In Hickory Grove, some people had crazy nicknames. She knew this solely based on the one vacation they had ever taken as a family. To Chicago, where people called their grandparents either Grandpa or Grandma. Where Williams could be Billies but nothing crazier than that.

In Hickory Grove, you could count on half the people you knew to go by something that didn't even hint at their given name.

Ky was a prime example. His real name was Hunter, as dictated by their father, but their mother went through a vegan phase that coincided with her fleeting adoration for all things islander, and well, Kai came up as some sort of temporary moniker, but then their daddy was filling out kindergarten registration paperwork and wrote Ky, and the rest was history.

Presently, everyone began talking at once, mostly about how they never did figure out if it was Lorna or Marguerite, despite the hard evidence in Mom's hands.

Then Mr. Rhett cleared his throat again and, speaking softly, asked, "What did she leave?"

Chapter 14 — Maggie

"The farmhouse," Maggie whispered. She drew her hand to her mouth. "*The farmhouse.*"

No one replied, giving her a moment to process. Even Briar, who had wiggled her way in between Maggie and Gretchen, just sat there, quiet and still.

Finally, Gretchen asked, "What farmhouse, Mom?"

Maggie's eyes flew to Rhett, who looked at her helplessly, and then back to Gretchen. "The Devereux Farmhouse. I thought it was condemned. Or that they sold it. Marguerite never told me..."

Gretchen gasped. "I know what you're talking about! She told me about it years ago. When I was little." The two women locked eyes. Maggie was well aware of the bond Gretchen thought she shared with the old spinster. The old woman who was good enough to take in Dirk and Maggie but bitter enough to keep things from them, too.

Like a real home. A motherly love. *Anything.*

"I've never been there. She told me it was far away and that there was nothing left but rotten wood and rusty farm equipment." Maggie's voice trailed off as memories rushed in. Her childhood longings for something more. Her teenaged wonderings over where she came from. Who her parents were. How the Devereux family got its start in town. Everyone had a history in Hickory Grove. How was Maggie so in the dark on her own? It seemed like a violation of a small town citizen's rights to not know her origins.

And what was more, no one else ever bothered to give her any insights. Even her best friend's own grandparents kept mum when it came to Devereux family lore.

And Fern Gale, sweet Fern Gale whose *job* it was to collect and document history, was entirely unaware of anything to do with the poor old Devereux clan who'd slowly but surely faded away, leaving behind just one of its own: Margaret Mary Devereux. Maggie. Who'd also forsaken her ancestral name in favor of a tattooed, big-rig-driving jerk named Travis Wayne Engel.

"Was Aunt Lorna your dad's sister or your mom's sister?" Dakota asked, his attention beginning to wane in favor of his comic book.

"My mom's," Maggie answered, slowly. "She was my mom's *aunt*."

"I thought Devereux was your dad's last name?" Ky asked.

"No. Some people think that because Marguerite was such a hermit. And she was a fibber," Maggie added lightly. "She liked to tell stories, and she would make things up and confuse people." Maggie pointed to the pages in her hands. "I guess that's why I'm bewildered."

"It would have been Dirk who'd set this up, right?" Rhett asked.

She nodded. "Right. He's on a rig right now. I haven't talked to him since the funeral."

"Did you know he was the executor?"

Maggie replied, "Yes. He handled the funeral entirely. But he never mentioned this."

"Maybe it was supposed to be a surprise," Gretchen reasoned.

"Maybe. The date is from three months ago. That would have been right after the service. Right before Dirk left." Maggie was working through the details in her mind.

"He probably figured the probate folks would settle it with you," Rhett offered, now moving toward Maggie. "May I look?"

"Yes, please." She passed him the documents and pulled Briar into a tight hug, kissing the little girl's flyaways into place along her temple.

"All you have to do is call this number," Rhett said at last, underlining an out-of-town series of digits with his index finger.

Maggie checked the time on her phone. "They'll be closed now," she answered.

"First thing in the morning," Gretchen said, a grin pushing her dimples high up on her cheeks. "Mom, I think we have a plan."

Chapter 15 — Rhett

Surely the paperwork didn't lie. Surely there existed some broken-down farmhouse from the 1800s, wasting away on the far side of Hickory Grove's town limits, just waiting for a desperate woman to take it over and turn it into cash, maybe.

But despite Rhett's distance in the last two decades, he knew Hickory Grove like the back of his hand, and this farmhouse had never made it on his radar, nor had anyone else in town ever mentioned any special property rotting out on the edge of civilization.

He took to his bedroom, had a shower, slipped back into his boxers, and dropped onto the bed. With no cellphone charger and few television channels, his only option was to lie awake in bed for some time and ruminate on life.

Emma came to mind but just as soon left. In place of thoughts of his long-term girlfriend, plans for the future flooded in. He hated to consider Hickory Grove a bust. But hope was lost. There was no point in making something out of nothing. Especially since the land was gone.

Visions of Louisville suffocated him. The traffic. The soulless world he'd been enduring—flipping house after house and all for what? Money? Cash he'd stuff away in his already potbellied checking account and 401K? Cash he'd never spend on a diamond ring or a college savings fund or a kitchen remodel for the woman with whom he'd toil over a Thanksgiving dinner?

Rhett wanted more from life. A family, sure. But was it too late?

A pickle. He was in a pickle.

Stay in Louisville and try to meet a new woman who would be willing to start a family with someone north of forty. Or: pick a small town and settle for a lonesome existence that would at least provide the community he'd missed for so long.

A knock came at the door. Rhett threw the covers back and, without thinking, strode to answer it.

No peephole in the door and no chain lock, so Rhett cracked it at first. Through the slit, peering tiredly into the darkness of his guest room stood Maggie.

Of course.

"Is everything okay?" he asked in hushed tones, glancing behind her down the hall.

Quickly, she averted her eyes. "I'm so sorry. Did I wake you?"

"No, no. Come in." He gestured her in and opened the door wider, but she froze in place, staring off to the right.

Rhett realized he was standing there almost naked. Laughing, he let the door fall shut somewhat. "Oh, jeez. I'm sorry. I'm used to—"

"Being naked?" she joked back, finally meeting his gaze, her hand catching the door and holding it for him.

He pulled it open wider. "Hang on," he told her, turning to find his jeans and tug them on.

Maggie let out a breath and entered his room, her arms crossed over her chest, shoulders hunched. "I'm so sorry. Really, I can go back."

"Oh, please. I could use the company. Can't sleep."

She nodded. "Same here."

"Want to talk about it?" he asked, sitting on his bed and patting the small space next to him.

"Not much to say," she admitted, easing herself down. They sat there, together, in silence for some time, until Maggie's weight shifted. Subtly. Comfortably. She cleared her throat. "I still can't get in touch with him."

Rhett's heart skipped a beat. He felt silly. Like a teenager again. A jealous teenager with a boyhood crush that would never resolve. He inched away. "Do you think he's still in town?"

"No, I don't. Someone would call me. It's Hickory Grove," she reasoned.

He nodded. "Do you think he'll come back?"

"No."

Again, silence.

Finally, Rhett asked, "Do you want him to?"

Maggie squeezed her eyes shut, but still a lone tear pushed its way out and down her cheek. Rhett was torn between keeping up the facade of decency and giving in to being a friend. Or more.

Her mouth stretched and she pushed the heels of her hands to her eyes, and the moment passed.

And in that moment, Rhett realized that the facade of decency was nothing more than a sheet of armor, protecting him from admitting that he had never stopped loving Maggie Devereux.

He swallowed hard, searching for the right thing to say. The good thing.

But it never came.

And soon enough, she rose and told him goodnight.

Dedicated to preserving what was left of that armor, he simply replied in kind, and locked his door.

Chapter 16 — Gretchen

The next morning, Gretchen woke up to a phone swollen with missed phone calls and text messages. The phone calls were all from Miss Becky. The texts, from Theo.

Carefully, without stirring Briar, she twisted under the covers and took to answering his many questions.

Yes, they were fine. Safe. *No*, they didn't need his help. *Yes*, she promised to call him if they *did* need his help.

But all that was for naught when, an hour later, a loud rap came at the door.

Standing just beyond it, was *not*, in fact, her mother clad in yesterday's outfit bringing over crusty bagels.

It was Theo himself. Tall, sinewy-limbed, dark-haired Theodore Linden. With two boxes of doughnuts teetering on one hand and a cardboard coffee carafe dangling from the other. "My mom is in your mom's room. She said I could come here first," he told Gretchen as she opened the door and waved him in.

The eighteen-year-old girl felt naked in her oversized t-shirt and threadbare boxer shorts—an old pair of her father's which now felt somehow meaningful and morbid all at once.

She had never stood in front of Theo without at least a smear of lip gloss and a coat of mascara.

This was a first in their friendship. Him seeing her like this. Jean-less. Makeup-less.

Homeless.

"How are you?" he asked, his face earnest. Underneath the boyishness of the college freshman there was something about Theo that was decidedly... manly. Gretchen wondered how that happened. How and when, exactly, a boy started to take the shape of a man.

Because even in her own father such a quality always seemed absent.

"Tired," Gretchen answered, pointing surreptitiously toward Briar who was now awake and doodling with focus on the back of an envelope Maggie had given her.

"Hi Briar," Theo offered the little girl. She pretended to ignore him, but a teensy smile curled up the edges of her pink mouth.

Gretchen rolled her eyes. "She's in love with you."

The Engels had only met Theo in the fall, but from there, he and Gretchen hit it off. As friends. Strictly.

He'd visited their house a few times and frequented Mally's whenever he knew Gretchen was working. They texted almost constantly.

But he'd be returning to Notre Dame in less than a week now. It was a better life for him, no doubt. Academia and heavy textbooks. Good instructors and a strong school parish. Little Flock was the only church Gretchen had ever known, but she hadn't known it much. Her parents rarely dragged everyone to mass. Though every last one of the Engel kids *was* baptized. That had never been negotiable. It was the one tradition Maggie had stood by no matter how little Travis had to do with it.

And Gretchen always clung to that early spiritual rite. It gave her something more than what she had. Something deeper. Intangible, perhaps. But *there*.

Currently, it struck her that she had no idea whether Theo was baptized. Not that it would matter. Would it? She shook her head.

"Thanks for the doughnuts," she offered, taking a glazed one to Briar before selecting a cinnamon twist for herself.

"No problem. Eat as much as you want," he added meaningfully as he stood there, boxes still awkwardly resting on his forearm. Theo's bicep twitched above the coffee box, and Gretchen chuckled.

"We're not starving," she said. "*Yet*," she added for comic effect, but Theo didn't laugh.

He searched the room for a spot to set the coffee, but there was none.

"Here, I'll take that." Gretchen reached for the cardboard handle. Her fingers brushed against his, and he fumbled to pass it over.

Once she positioned it carefully on the bed, she offered him a seat on the chair next to the window. Suddenly, the room felt a little less like a jail cell and a little more like the bed-and-breakfast it was advertised as. Speaking of which, it occurred to her that the owners might be serving a delicious breakfast just then, as she was chewing into a pastry.

Oh well. She'd rather have Theo's treat anyway.

"You know, Gretchen," he started, glancing furtively toward the distracted child on the bed. "You're crazy not to stay with us. It could be... fun. To have you there."

Gretchen blinked. Her joke from before disappeared and with it any humor. And at last, grief fell over her. A powerful, humiliating grief. Never in her life had she been reliant on handouts. Her parents had provided well for them, and neither Gretchen nor her siblings had ever wanted for anything. All that, perhaps, added to her mortification at Theo's innocent and kind offer. Uncomfortable, she stood from her seat on the bed. "Thanks again, Theo. I'm sure the boys are starving. Why don't you take the doughnuts over to them?"

Embarrassed too, Theo rose and nodded urgently. "Right, sure. Sorry, I'll go."

And, he did.

Gretchen strode to the bathroom, tore off a length of toilet paper, wrapped the rest of her doughnut in it and tossed the whole sticky mess into the trash. Then she rummaged into her makeup bag until she found her mascara and proceeded to add four thick, black layers.

Chapter 17 — Maggie

One night at the Inn wasn't enough to convince Maggie to stay with Becky. Even if they were cramped together in two tiny rooms. Her pride was still too great.

And now, the little group of five had an out. A place.

Maybe... a home.

It was too soon to tell, and Becky had to go to work.

Theo disappeared on them after dropping the doughnuts off, and Gretchen began to pout, curiously enough. Especially when Rhett Houston appeared in front of Maggie's room soon after Becky and Theo had left.

"It's Mr. Houston," Gretchen called back to her mother, who was five minutes into the luke-warmest shower of her life.

Despite the distinctly uncomfortable feeling of a shower that was far too short of steaming hot, Maggie's anxiety had ebbed that morning, what with the second offer of a place to stay and the reassurance that she had something to do that day. Namely, learn more about this supposed farmhouse.

She killed the water, dabbed her skin dry, and pulled on a fresh pair of yoga pants and a thermal sweater before popping her head out to discover Rhett was not inside the room but rather out waiting in the hall.

"You four get dressed and ready. We're leaving in about five minutes," she directed, aiming her phone at Briar who couldn't seem to resist the box of paperwork.

"Hey," Maggie said to Rhett, whose tall frame leaned into the wall.

"Hey," he replied, combing his hand through his hair. "Sorry to interrupt you all, but I just wanted to check in on you. And," he began, searching for his next sentence.

Maggie found it for him. "You want your truck back."

His lips formed a line, half smile and half apology. "Yep."

"I already called Gunner this morning. He's going to open the shop without Travis. Your truck should be done by the afternoon." She smiled at Rhett, whose face lit up.

"Thank you *so* much, Maggie," he replied earnestly. "I really didn't want to ride in a tow truck down the Ohio back to the city.

"I don't blame you," she answered. "And, Rhett, I am *so* sorry it even came to this." She gestured around herself at the bed-and-breakfast.

Rhett pushed off the wall and shoved his hands in his jeans pockets, then faced her fully, his face impassive, his voice quiet. "I'm not."

Chapter 18 — Rhett

Maggie invited him along to the farmhouse, and Rhett wanted to go. Firstly, because he was curious about this mystery locale, tucked away in the woods off of County Road 131. Secondly, because he didn't want to *not* be around Maggie.

Rhett Houston had come to Hickory Grove with a goal to reconnect with his past. And here she was. In the hotel room next to his.

Letting his one true friend from high school slip back through his fingers would be criminal, really.

But there was Emma. And Travis. And that veneer of decency that only thickened as the drama intensified.

Anyway, none of this was about romance. Romance was the furthest thing from Rhett's mind. It was about spending time with people he cared about. And Rhett never had stopped caring about Maggie Devereux. Even if she became Maggie Engel.

Even if she always stayed that way.

However, he was a good man first and foremost. So, when Maggie and the kids were scrambling down the stairs ahead of him, he made his decision.

And it would mean that once his tire was changed, he wouldn't stick around Hickory Grove one minute longer.

"WHERE ARE YOU?" EMMA'S voice hissed across the line, and Rhett wondered if she'd somehow tracked him to the outer edge of Hickory Grove. She sounded close. And cold. The contradiction wasn't lost on him.

He'd stepped away to take the phone call, which killed him as Maggie and the kids spilled out of the SUV and stood on the corner of the woods, facing a creaking, sprawling property the likes of which Rhett could hardly have imagined.

"Emma, I'm with an old friend. Maggie Devereux. Dirk's sister, remember?"

His girlfriend snarled into his ear, "You didn't do the dishes yesterday. Did you get my *text*?"

Rhett cringed. "I'm sorry. I—you're right." He did feel a little bad. The one job he had was to empty the dishwasher, an irritating task at best. A fight-inducing task at worst. And a fragile, failing relationship was the exact context for *the worst*.

"When are you coming home?" Emma's voice softened, but not enough.

"Truck'll be done this afternoon. I'm helping Maggie with something while I wait."

"I'm having the girls over tonight for Bunco; don't forget. Which is *why* I needed you to do the dishes. I'm not nagging you, Rhett."

Rhett eyed the Engel family as they slowly ascended on the property. "I know, and I'm sorry. I'll be home as soon as I can. I promise."

Emma pushed a huff through the phone. "Well, actually, we were hoping to have the place to ourselves."

"For *Bunco*?" Rhett asked, ever confused by the life of a thirty-something who'd never married or had children. The life of his own girlfriend. A girlfriend *he* had never had the desire to, well, marry or have children with. "Listen, I *am* coming back tonight, because you and I need to talk. Okay?"

"On *Bunco* night? Wait a minute, wait a minute. Are you... are you going to *break up* with me?"

Rhett felt his heart stop at the suggestion, and it was only then that he realized that, yes. He was. But certainly not over the phone. And probably *not* during Bunco night.

"Actually, this is perfect. Wow, this is *so* totally *perfect*, Rhett." Her voice grew louder. "I'm done. I'm so *totally* done. You want to break up? You win. I'm done. I'll pack your closet tomorrow. Don't bother to come home. No reason."

A click concluded the call, and Rhett figured he had no say. But it was just as well. After all, he had no interest in crashing a Bunco party.

And he certainly had no interest in seeing Emma ever again.

A wave of relief washed over him, breaking up the knots in his neck, assuaging his upset stomach. His spine miraculously straightened. Though he felt not an ounce of guilt or displeasure, Rhett wondered if he ought to.

But then his eyes fell on Maggie. Her blonde-streaked hair whipped across her face, revealing the red underneath, as she turned from the foot of the front deck to search for him. Briar spotted him first and waved wildly with the passion and innocence of a little girl who grew up in a small town. His small town. And then Rhett wished so badly that the Houston family land was still available. Because if it were, he'd start building a house that very night. He'd lay down his roots right then and there.

It wasn't, though. And Rhett realized that soon enough he'd have to move into one of his rentals in Louisville. Start over. Make the right decisions this time.

No more younger women.

No more property flips.

It was time for Rhett Houston to get serious about his future. If he wanted a family, if he wanted what Maggie Engel had, no matter how she came about it, he'd better get to work.

Chapter 19 — Maggie

Maggie spied Rhett shove his phone into his jeans and stride toward her, albeit slowly. He took in the house just as she had moments ago. Part of her wished Becky was here. Or Fern. Dirk. Someone she was close with to share in this jaw-dropping moment.

The first jaw-dropping moment she'd had ever since she found out she was pregnant with Gretchen.

But when Rhett grew nearer and she could make out the expression on his face—the warmth... the awe... the *happiness* for her, she felt better. As though she had the exact right person at that moment. Apparently, it didn't matter that he'd been gone for so long. Apparently, theirs was a genuine friendship that had withstood the test of time. Among other things.

"Maggie, wow. How did we miss this place?"

Briar wriggled loose and begged her mom to go wander inside with her older siblings. Maggie grabbed Briar's hand before she slipped away. "Not alone," she answered before hollering for Ky to come and escort his little sister on her adventure through the ramshackle house. "Watch out for nails," she called after them.

Rhett added, "And loose floorboards." Maggie smiled at him gratefully. "Don't you want to go in?" he asked.

She shook her head. "I need to stand here for a minute. Figure out the answer to your question and take it all in. You know?"

He nodded by her side.

They were quiet for a few beats. A patient quiet. If it were Travis standing with Maggie, he'd rush her through a cursory inspection then ask if they could go eat lunch. He was like a child, really. Only now, in the presence of a real man, did Maggie recognize that.

Staring up at the house, she realized it seemed bigger from the road. Back there, the faded wood siding appeared to disappear into the trees behind it. Now, as she stood at the foot of the front deck—a sizable front deck for the time period, no doubt—she realized the place was probably smaller than her current (or rather, former) home. That might be a good thing.

The exterior, at one time, had to have been white. Now pale gray, splotches of discoloration spread from between the second-story windows and the corners where the walls met each other at almost-but-not-quite-perfect ninety-degree angles. No railing existed on the edges of the deck, which gave a sort of looming effect to the whole thing.

Weeds and trees grew into the house, shielding it from the highway and even from its own road. No drive or path had been apparent when Maggie stumbled across a wooden pole that once might have held a mailbox. That, coupled with the general area, was her only clue that she might find what she was looking for.

And so they had. Found what they were looking for, that was.

"When did your aunt live here?" Rhett asked, stepping away to size up a barn that sat sinking directly into the earth off behind the house.

Maggie shook her head as she thought about the answer. "Not during my lifetime. It wasn't my aunt's, actually," she said. "It was my grandparents'. And their parents before, if you can believe that."

Rhett strode back to her and climbed the steps. He held his hand out to support her as she took cautious steps up. The wood sagged beneath their combined weight, and she squeezed his hand out of necessity.

He squeezed back.

Maggie's heart pounded in her chest. The farmhouse. The circumstances. Her hand in Rhett's.

It was too much. Once they reached the front door, she softly tugged herself free of him, crossing her arms over her chest to brace against a whipping wind that came out of nowhere.

Rhett stuck his hands in his pockets and peered in through the gaping door, unfazed by the moment they'd just shared. "I just can't believe this place hasn't been tagged to oblivion. Or that no one has been living out here. Maybe they have."

At that, Maggie's heart raced yet again. Suddenly panicked, she cried out, "Gretchen! Dakota! Ky! Get back here *now*!"

The four kids scrambled around the side of the house, panting with excitement. "This place is amazing, Mom," Gretchen gushed as though she were closer to Ky's age. The other three nodded with exaggeration by her side.

"Okay, well, just be careful, alright? Stay together. We don't know what's going on here."

The kids agreed and ambled off again, leaving Maggie and Rhett to enter the house, at last.

Maggie wasn't much for sentimentality, but something told her to savor the experience. After all, the more time she spent there, assessing the property and studying the project, the less time she had to worry about her undelivered divorce paperwork. Or where her husband was. Or what was becoming of the only other house she'd ever known.

Rhett stayed to the far side of the front door, allowing Maggie to enter first.

The inside was, surprisingly, in better shape than the outside.

Rotted and withered in some spots, sure, but better.

The front door opened into a narrow foyer with a staircase to the second floor. Hardwood peaked out beneath worn-down rubbery squares. Maggie tapped her foot on the dusty white. "Linoleum?" she asked Rhett.

He shrugged. "Maybe your grandparents had it updated?"

At that, they both chuckled. "Easy to keep up, I guess," she murmured, turning left into what must have been a parlor or living room. Maybe both. Early Hickory Grove settlers who'd arrived by way of France likely struggled to strike a balance between pragmatism and old-country opulence.

What surprised her was the in-tactness of it all. It was like a movie. A haunted-house movie. Sheets and plastic draped over the low-profile furniture. As she lifted the dry-rot plastic, Maggie detected one sofa and two sitting chairs. On the floor between them spanned a rug, which had largely dissolved, though due to what elements was unclear. For a snowy few days, the interior of the house felt dry and preserved. Much like a tomb. Chilly, yes, but dry.

It reminded her of Marguerite, and she shuddered.

"I wonder why Dirk didn't put up a fight for this place," Maggie mused aloud.

Rhett, who'd wandered off in the opposite direction, called her over to a back room.

Maggie passed through a second doorway and found him in a tight dining room space.

Missing from the boxy area was a table, but four weathered dining chairs lined the far wall, as if waiting for a party. Through the far doorway of that space was the kitchen.

She swallowed and tried to quell her nervous energy as she entered the kitchen. With a good vacuuming and a few coats of wax, it would be something out of a modern-day catalogue, meant to convince an upper-middle-class family that down-home chic was still *in*.

A once-white apron sink sat squarely along the back wall in the center of a wooden countertop. At the far side, a shapely Frigidaire taunted Maggie. Reading her mind, Rhett tried to open it, but it was stuck shut, as though the rubber seal had melted into glue. "I can pull harder, but I'm afraid I'll..."

His voice trailed off, and their attention turned to a pot-bellied stove on the adjacent wall. On top, a cast-iron pan, rusted over entirely.

"I can't get over it," Maggie whispered. "It's like a museum or something."

Something dawned on her. "Hold on," she said to Rhett. "If anyone knows anything about this place and why it's just sitting here, preserved like a mummy, it'll be Fern."

Rhett asked, "Are you talking about Fern Monroe?" His eyes grew wide. He remembered her, apparently. The odd girl who'd been homeschooled. The one who seemed fifty years older than them while they were children. She wasn't even five years older, in fact.

"Yeah," Maggie answered, her phone to her ear.

Fern answered after the first ring. "Maggie, are you okay?"

"Yes, I'm fine. Fern, listen. I have a big question for you. Huge, really. There's a lot to explain, but basically, did you know about my family's farmhouse out on County Road 131? The old Devereux place, apparently?"

Fern sighed before launching into a long, winding story. Maggie signaled to Rhett that he could go look around as she settled in to listen.

Chapter 20 — Gretchen

"**W**hat did she say?" Gretchen asked Maggie. They had all gathered in the kitchen. Briar and Gretchen had just finished examining the upstairs. Three bedrooms. Small, but still. One bathroom—or at least, that's what she assumed it was meant to be. There was no toilet, and Gretchen found it hard to believe that a house with linoleum floors and a refrigerator didn't have indoor plumbing.

Then again, Dakota was swearing up and down he found an outhouse. "A real, live outhouse! With a padlock!"

"Yeah," Ky chimed in. "The barn was locked too. I couldn't even see inside." Sadness filled his voice, almost suddenly, before he went on. "Dad could probably break the lock. Let's try calling him again."

Their mom offered a sympathetic smile and scruffed Ky's hair. "We'll call him again. I promise."

"Mom," Gretchen pressed, attempting both to garner more information from Miss Fern and also to distract her brother. "What did Miss Fern say?"

Gretchen saw Rhett inch toward her mom, and it made her feel queasy. The whole thing was nauseating—getting booted from their home, her useless father running off, a sleepless night in a hotel room, meeting this *stranger* who acted like he was best friends with her mother. She tried to ignore their proximity as Maggie began to share.

The farmhouse was vacated just months before Maggie was born. All of the Devereuxs lived there. Mimi and Papa Devereux, Camille (Maggie's mother) and Marguerite, too. Then, one day, just months before the twins were born, something happened, Miss Fern said. According to Mrs. Monroe, Miss Fern's mother, the Devereuxs sent Camille to a boarding house for young ladies. Marguerite stayed behind, but then something *else* happened, and they put the farmhouse up for sale.

Hickory Grove being what it was—no one made an offer. Months passed, and during that time, Mimi and Papa slowly sold off their livestock. Papa took a position as custodian at Hickory Grove High. Mimi took up work at the seamstress' house, teaching and training Marguerite as her replacement when Marguerite wasn't caring for her dead sister's newborn twins.

"So what happened to your mom?" Gretchen asked Maggie, saddened to hear the strange story, and curious about why the family would give up a perfectly good farm. Even in the wake of their daughter's untimely death.

Much to everyone's shock, Maggie's eyes teared up and her mouth stretched into the beginnings of a sob. Alarmed, Gretchen crossed to her mother and wrapped her in a hug.

Rhett stood nearby, awkwardly patting Maggie's back.

Briar burst out wailing. Ky choked up. Dakota muttered under his breath that he'd rather be at school after all.

Everyone sort of gave Maggie a moment to recover. Her chest still heaving, she covered her mouth with her hand and tried to continue. "I never spoke about it, because they never told us. I didn't even know. I can't believe I didn't know. They never told us," she began.

Gretchen frowned. "Who never told you? Never told you what?"

"No one told us, but I always figured it might be the case," their mom answered, shuddering through the tail end of her flash sob session.

"About your mom, you mean?" Rhett pinned Gretchen's mother with a sympathetic stare, and it seemed to work.

"She went into labor at the boarding house. The nuns weren't prepared. It happened fast. First Dirk. Then me. She didn't run away like I thought. She gave birth to us. Then..."

"What, Mom?" Gretchen asked, grabbing the woman's writhing hands and squeezing them together in place to quiet her. "Then what?"

Calmly staring through the children, her gaze fixed on nothing, Maggie whispered her reply. "She didn't make it. My mom died. Right there in that boarding house across the river. She died."

Chapter 21 — Rhett

Rhett's parents were dead, too. And they were young, too. But nothing quite as dramatic as Maggie's situation. His mother had cancer. Twice. That she beat it the first time set their expectations too high for round two.

His father had a heart attack just weeks after his wife's funeral. A shock to him and everyone. No matter how many times a person beat cancer, her death would always be hard. They always were.

Death was like that. Traumatic. Something you never recovered from. Losing a loved one grew easier with time, sure. But it left a little hole in your heart. One that could never be sewn closed with a neat stitch. It was just there. Exposing your insides and turning you vulnerable. Sending a choking feeling to your throat. Giving you a headache or making you cry on a perfectly usual day years later.

So for Maggie to learn about—and then have to relay—her own mother's death (and the circumstances surrounding it) was difficult to be part of.

But he was there. He was committed. And not because his truck was tied up with some goofball understudy at the garage. Not because Emma broke up with him. Not because he came back to Hickory Grove to head down to the brewery with Luke or Dirk or any other number of old buddies. Not even because he thought he had a claim to some land.

Rhett Houston was there, at that farmhouse, with Maggie and her pitiful children, because it's where God needed him to be.

After another round of hugs, things settled, and Maggie asked aloud what they ought to do next.

Gretchen, in spite of herself, began to ramble on about fixing up the farmhouse and living there. Dakota and Ky were equally enthusiastic, their early concern for their mother quickly washed away by the suggestion that they might get to live smack dab in the middle of the woods. Images of Daniel Boone flashed through Rhett's mind's eye and he recalled a time when he'd have liked to live farther out of town. A time when he wanted to explore areas unknown.

Briar had started complaining of hunger, and Maggie was losing focus fast.

Rhett cleared his throat. "How about we break for lunch then you can come back and finish looking around?"

Maggie glanced up at him. "Lunch sounds good. But won't you have to leave soon?"

Color rushed up Rhett's neck, and—despite the frigid weather—his palms grew slick. He shoved his hands into his pockets and sucked in a breath. "Well, I, ah—actually, I have to make some phone calls myself. And, I figured you'd probably want time to sort through all this as a—ah, you know—as a family?" He finished by scratching the back of his head and sort of twisting away, awkwardly as ever. He felt sixteen all over again. Gretchen's eyes were on him. His neck flushed deeper.

"Oh, okay," Maggie replied, her tired face falling. "Well, first join us for lunch. Won't you?"

"If it's okay with everyone," he replied, lifting his eyebrows to the oldest children. Ky and Dakota all but ignored him. Gretchen, he could have sworn, rolled her eyes.

But Briar, sweet Briar, shrieked at the top of her lungs, raced to Rhett and wrapped her little body around his legs.

Apparently, hers was the opinion that mattered most, because soon enough, they were off toward Mally's.

Where it all began.

SIX BURGERS, THREE chocolate milks, two diet sodas, and one sweet tea later, the motley crew was poised to leave.

Rhett paid the bill, swiftly negating Maggie's protests, and then they found themselves at the SUV once again. He hadn't received a call about his truck yet, but now he was just down the street from the garage.

He jutted his chin up Main Street. "I'm going to go check in on the truck. See if it's done."

The kids were in the car, except for Gretchen, who stood whispering into her phone a few paces away.

Maggie tore her attention from her oldest daughter, sighing with a smile. "Young love," she said to Rhett, shaking her head. "Or whatever that is." She hooked a thumb back toward Gretchen.

Rhett frowned. "She's dating that kid? Becky's son?"

"No. I wish she would."

He chuckled. "Sounds familiar."

Maggie lifted an arched eyebrow. "Familiar?"

"Come on, Maggie, don't you remember? My mom always nagged me to ask you out." A younger Rhett would have been embarrassed at the admission. But they were old enough now that it was a light memory. Nothing more. "I was too scared. You were too pretty," he confessed, meeting her eyes.

The wind seemed to shut off, and the cold air around them grew a little thicker. "Are you still?" Maggie answered, staring hard at Rhett.

His tongue passed over his lower lip and he fell back half a step, his stomach dipping a little. "Maggie Devereux, are you asking if I'm still *scared*?"

"It's Engel to you, Rhett Houston."

Their banter turned serious. "That's true. My apologies," he replied, looking away. "Maggie Engel." He cleared his throat. All through elementary school and junior high, they were strangers. Then high school hit, and a bond formed. And even as Maggie started dating Travis, the joking didn't ebb. People accused Maggie and Rhett of liking each other. Whatever that meant. She brushed it off easily, to his disappointment. And then, Travis entered the picture, and Rhett told himself he'd moved on anyway.

"What if I'm not?" The question sort of fell out of his mouth. Rough and low.

Maggie scrunched her face and leaned toward him. "What if you're not *what*?"

Rhett took a step toward her, licked his lips, and pushed his hands deeper into his pockets, a fresh burst of wind curling around them, pressing them together. "What if I'm not scared anymore?"

Chapter 22 — Maggie

If only Maggie and Rhett had held back after walking out of Mally's. Turned right as the kids turned left. They could be in an alley, wrapped in each other's arms, making up for lost time and missed chances.

She would kiss him. In another time. Another place. Without her kids watching from behind the windshield. Without Gretchen struggling nearby with her own emotions over a fuzzy cell phone connection. Without a... *husband*.

But Maggie was an adult now, suffering the consequences of her hesitation to file for a divorce. She could kick herself. Presently, with the harshness of retrospect, she didn't understand her own choices.

Why hadn't she filed weeks ago? Months ago? *Years* ago? Right after Briar's birth, when Travis went to the bar to "celebrate" while Maggie lay propped in a hospital bed, struggling for the fourth time to get her newborn to breastfeed. Worrying about giving up and giving into bottles (when had "bottle" become a bad word, anyway?). Worrying about Gretchen once again standing in as a mother for Ky and Dakota. Worrying that it was all a mistake but remembering that none of it was.

Which was true. Because even though she wanted to push off the pavement and press her mouth into Rhett's and she could not, would not do that, life was almost perfect.

Four beautiful children.

A house that could *be* a home.

One of her old best friends who, maybe, loved her. Even if it was just a platonic love.

But everything needed to come together. And the one thing that would bring it together was good decision-making. For once.

"Come with me," she blurted out.

Rhett frowned. "To the farmhouse?"

"To the bank," she answered. "Then the attorney's office. Come with me. Help me. Please, Rhett. Won't you?" She stared into his eyes, searching for his answer.

He sighed. "I'd love to, Maggie, but—"

"Oh my," she replied, her hand over her mouth. "*You're* probably married. Oh, Rhett. How could I... I never asked. You're... married, aren't you? I'm so stupid, I—" Her estrangement from Travis suddenly dissipated. None of it mattered if Rhett had someone. And why wouldn't he? Muscular and tall. Kind and hardworking. Rhett, she realized for the first time in her life, was a great catch.

"No, no, no," he replied, holding his hands up. "No, I'm single, actually. Recently single. Never married. No kids. I'm free, in fact, but you're—"

A grin spread across her mouth and she glanced back to the kids. Gretchen, who'd apparently ended her phone call, had loaded herself into the front seat of the SUV. "We'll give you a ride up to the garage. It's too cold to stand out here a moment longer."

He did as he was told, pulling himself into the second seat as Dakota climbed into the far back. Rhett apologized, but Dakota didn't seem to mind.

Ky, on the other hand, bore a hole through the rearview mirror at Maggie.

"Where are we going?" he huffed from the far back.

"Dropping Mr. Rhett at his truck then running errands. We're settling everything *to-day*," she replied, stabbing her index finger on each syllable.

Gretchen peered out of the corner of her eye at her mother. "What's 'everything'?"

IT HAD BEEN EXACTLY one day almost down to the hour. One day since she arrived home to a thin, pink sheet. One day since she emergency-packed and threw the kids in the SUV. One day since she overreacted.

Now there she was, back at their home on Pine Tree Lane.

Everything sat exactly how it had the day before with one exception.

A *For Sale* sign. Shoved deep into the cold, soggy earth next to her mailbox. Courtesy of the bank.

Travis had been in touch with the manager overseeing their "case" before she'd even arrived. All she had to do was sign. Give it up. For good.

There was no other option. Travis made that painfully clear in a pointed text message. The only one she would ever receive from him. All future correspondence, he claimed, could go through his mother. But that was fine, and she was grateful he'd answered at last.

The message had offered a one-word apology, if you could call it that. No justification or explanation. Simply an incomplete sentence about meeting someone else and figuring things out.

She had tapped out a message about the kids, a divorce, and custody plans then quickly deleted it. Instead, she screenshot his words, texted the picture to Becky and asked Becky to send it to Zack Durbin, Esquire. Then, she sent a new response, requesting his new address.

He never replied.

Maggie had to force herself from wondering if he ever would. Part of her would much rather have a blow-out fight than silence... or wondering.

But it was out of her control now. And she had two weeks to empty the house, per the arrangement with the bank.

So there they were: an exhausted Maggie. An irritable Gretchen. Two wound-up pre-teen boys. And one snoring preschooler.

Rhett was negotiating at the garage with Travis's underlings who, instead of simply changing out the tire, took it upon themselves to rebuild his front end for some reason unknown to everyone. Maggie offered to stay with him to talk some sense into the grease monkeys, but he refused, telling her they would reconnect after she took the kids back to the house to take a break.

Perhaps Rhett needed a break from them, too. After all, he ended up joining her on her errands, acting as something of a translator for Maggie who tried but failed to keep her emotions in check in front of the business-faced bank manager who explained the circumstances of the foreclosure and also revealed that Travis had everything (everything—as in he showed up to sign off on some documents) in order for a smooth transition.

His parting gift, Maggie thought sadly. A smooth transition from having a perfectly good home to almost nothing, save for the oddly preserved farmhouse on the outskirts of town.

But Travis didn't know about the farmhouse.

Where did he think Maggie and the kids would live? Oh, right. With his mother, who had called Maggie no fewer than a dozen times in the past hour leaving accusatory voicemails and terse texts. It seemed she'd learned about her rotten son and made the decision his actions were a result of Maggie's weak efforts at wifehood. Even so, the woman tacked on to the end of each message that Maggie and the kids could come stay with her *until they fixed their little problem.* Mrs. Engel's callous attempt at grace.

Grace, however, would not be huddling together in that harsh woman's house where children were not allowed to touch anything and where it would be indecent for Maggie to share a bed with her grown daughter (as had been the accusation years before when the house was fumigated and the family had their first experience as house guests in that cramped three-bedroom. Mrs. Engel clucked her tongue when Travis called at eleven at night to say he'd just stay with a buddy to save them the space. So instead of letting Gretchen and Briar squeeze onto the sofa, Maggie invited them into her bed. Mrs. Engel fumed at the "odd" choice and offered them all the silent treatment for breakfast.)

Grace.

Grace was her inheritance.

And, of course, there was Rhett Houston, too. Single. In town on some sort of trip down memory lane. Kind and happy to help a mom in distress.

Too bad Maggie would never date again. Not even if she wanted to kiss him or anyone else in the whole wide world. For Maggie, romance was officially a thing of the past. As for now, she needed to get her act together.

Chapter 23 — Gretchen

Theo was blowing up her phone. Her joy over the farmhouse was his, too. Her stress over returning to their home was his stress, too. And her thick hatred for her father was Theo's mission.

"You can't just take it lying down," he whispered to her as they lounged in her bedroom—her almost former bedroom—upstairs. Briar was taking a late nap. The boys were zoning out to TV. Her mom was packing, and Gretchen knew that any minute Maggie would appear in her doorway, hands on hips, acid on her tongue that Gretchen *better get her butt downstairs and help, now!*

She turned to face Theo, who sat in her desk chair. A third of a scarf sat on her lap, its dutiful crochet hook in her right hand, yarnless for now. She'd been overjoyed to find the project that she'd been frantically searching for the day before. "What do you mean? We aren't taking anything lying down? We're packing and moving," she replied evenly.

"I mean your mom should sue him or something. Or have a cop find him and drag him back here to... to..."

"To what, Theo? Men leave their wives and families all the time. My mom's dad left. Your dad left. They leave." It was a great opportunity to give Theo a meaningful look, or even a searching one. But Gretchen couldn't stand to lock eyes.

"Don't become a husband and father. It does something to men," she added lightly, jabbing her hook into the end of a row on the scarf, pinching the line of yarn with the other hand, and wrapping it into place with a sigh of satisfaction.

"My dad didn't leave," Theo replied, standing from his seat. "My parents split up. Remember? Or are you too focused on your own drama?"

Gretchen looked up from her lap, shocked, to see Theo turn and leave the room. "Theo, wait!" she called.

Though he didn't turn around, his long legs slowed to a stop at the beginning of the hallway.

Obviously she was focused on her own drama. How dare he suggest that she was being selfish? And anyway, his life was literally perfect. Before he walked away again, she inhaled a sharp breath then spat, "Yeah I'm focused on my own drama. Because *I* actually *have* some. There is literally nothing wrong in your life, Theodore Linden. You've got it all." He began to turn, and she snapped her mouth shut. Too far. She'd taken it way too far.

"I'm sorry," she began, meeting his soft gaze.

But he didn't seem angry. He seemed sad. "I've got it all? That's what you think?" he began, turning to face her fully, his arms crossed over his chest.

Gretchen swallowed hard and peered at him, shaking her head slowly. She'd never seen Theo like this. Take-charge and brusque. Defiant and steely-eyed. Her skin prickled and her blood pooled in her chest, making breathing harder work than it had been just moments before.

Theo shook his head, too, mimicking her. "You're right, Gretchen. And I'm sorry you're going through this. You're right. Life is easier for me right now. But I can promise you one thing. I don't have it all. Because I don't have *you*."

And with that, he turned and left.

Gretchen heard him stomp down the staircase, say something to her mother, and then fade into the echoing chambers of the downstairs.

It never occurred to her that Theo liked her.

Mostly, it never occurred to her that she liked him back.

Chapter 24 — Rhett

Rhett had just passed Theo on his way out of the house. The boy's face turned away, his hands deep in his coat pockets, his feet hitting the walkway with a purpose.

Maggie stood in the doorway, her hands on her hips, hair piled high on her head in a messy bun. Amusement filled her clean, freckled face.

"What's going on?" Rhett began to ask, but his question was quickly answered when Gretchen, barefoot despite the frost, tore past her mother, down the porch, and nearly tackled Theo.

Rhett and Maggie watched together as Theo turned, bewildered at Gretchen's surprise attack but fast-thinking, scooped her up off the sidewalk. Before Rhett could find out where the bizarre show of affection was coming from—or where it was going—Maggie tugged him inside.

"Wow," she said once they were safely behind a closed front door. Mischief played across her features contagiously. Rhett smiled back.

"What was *that* all about?" he asked, suddenly aware that Maggie was still holding onto his hand. Aware that Ky and Dakota were standing at the bottom of her stairs watching.

"What's going on?" Ky asked, accusation in his voice.

Maggie dropped Rhett's hand. "Nothing." She shook her head. "Well, Gretchen and Theo," she went on. "Oh, nothing. Don't worry about it. Gretchen is outside with Theo. That's all." She flicked a glance up at Rhett then back to her sons. "Why don't you two take a break from TV and start working on your room. Two weeks, remember?" She clapped her hands up at them, and they scrambled off obediently but not before Ky turned his head to Rhett, a frown set across his little mouth.

Clearing his throat, Rhett told Maggie that his truck was done, front end and all, for the price of a new tire. Time to get going. He had to return to Louisville.

Her smile faded then lit back up. "Wait! Before you go. I want to... show you something," she said, nodding her head toward the kitchen.

Once they were there, Maggie scooped her phone from the table and held the screen to his face.

A green box with a long text exchange glowed at him.

The name of the sender: Zack Durbin, their old pal from high school—Becky's high school sweetheart, in fact. He'd become a local lawyer. For the school district mainly, but he'd recently taken over his father's formerly defunct law firm.

"What does this mean?" he asked Maggie, finding himself all of a sudden uncomfortable with a window into her personal affairs. Too close to the fire. Then again, he had been for the past twenty-four hours. Maybe it was too late. Maybe Rhett already *was* involved in her personal affairs.

Actually, he *hoped* he was.

She blinked. "It means Zack is going to help me. *Pro bono.* Becky stopped by and picked up the paperwork I filled out. If Travis and I are both willing to file amicably and we get the paperwork in and do the settlement conference and parenting classes, then wait sixty days..." She stopped for a breath. "I'm free. *We're* free. The kids and me, I mean." She added the last part to quell his discomfort, no doubt. Maybe her own, too.

"Will you get alimony? Child support?" It was an intrusive question, and he didn't deserve an answer. He held up his hand and began to excuse himself, but she answered.

"If I don't request it, then things will go more smoothly. As far as we know, Travis doesn't even have a job anymore. He could be living on the streets, even."

Rhett frowned. "Maggie, you stayed at home for a while, right? I mean, won't you need some financial support? Don't you want it?"

She shook her head. "I have the farmhouse. I have my clients. I can do it. And I can do it *alone*, if I have to, Rhett."

He nodded slowly. "Alone."

They locked eyes briefly, before Maggie replied, "Will you come back?"

"You mean to Hickory Grove?"

"Yeah. Since your land is gone, are you still moving back?"

Rhett swallowed. "I'm not sure. I'll talk to Luke and see if that lot by him is up for sale. I want to, Maggie." He stared hard at her. "I'd love to be back. Closer to Greta, for one. And I'm sick of the city, but—"

"But what?" she pressed.

He shrugged. "It doesn't make sense. I had a plan, but it didn't work out. Maybe it's God's way of saying I'm better off somewhere else. Closer to my rentals, for one."

"Right," she answered quietly. "I understand."

A moment passed between them during which they could hear the boys upstairs arguing. Briar's pipsqueak voice chimed in at intervals, and Rhett realized that even though he'd spent only a day with the Engel family, he was going to miss them. Maybe they'd miss him, too. Well, except for Ky. He opened his mouth to ask about that only to realize he knew the answer. "I'd better go. Before Ky challenges me to a brawl," he added playfully.

Maggie smiled. "Ky has always been my quiet one. Suspicious, too, I suppose. He's not quick to love. But when he does, well, he's all in. Maybe one day you two will find common ground."

Rhett nodded, wistful. "I'd like that. Maggie, I've really enjoyed my visit. I mean, I know it's probably been the worst twenty-four hours of your life, but—" he cracked a smile and felt stupid for pointing out his joy against her hardship, but Maggie just smiled.

"Come back to Hickory Grove, okay Rhett?" She moved a step closer to him, rose on the balls of her feet, braced herself against his chest, and gave him a peck on the cheek before whispering, "Come back soon."

Chapter 25 — Rhett

A week had passed since his half-baked effort to move to Hickory Grove, but in that time a lot had happened. Emma, true to her word, had everything from his rarely worn tie pins to his barbecue utensils bagged and tagged and sitting by the front door with a note that told him to come back for his tools while she was at work.

The lonely ordeal made him feel a little homeless, though not as much as Maggie might have been feeling.

Part of his depression stemmed from just how little Rhett realized truly belonged to him. As a stable sort of guy, he felt naked to be reduced to one suitcase and three garbage bags. Then again, he'd been all too happy to allow Emma to sell off his small appliances and bachelor furniture before she let him move in with her.

He spent another three days in a hotel until one of his tenants, whose lease wasn't up until the following month, called to say they were unable to pay rent and therefore vacating early. When he drove down to meet the well-intentioned college drop-out who had been living in Rhett's University-area studio unit, he could tell the kid must have bounced weeks back. The place was barren.

But he collected the key and bid farewell—no hard feelings but no returned deposit—and promptly set up camp.

Rhett kept about half of his rental units furnished—all of the ones that were generally sought after by the University set. With fresh sheets and a good scrub down, he could stick around the studio for as long as it took to find somewhere more... *permanent* for himself.

After he finished cleaning the unit and running to the store for the bare essentials, he gave Greta a call.

She answered the phone cheerily and after a brief greeting and the usual small talk, Rhett hit her with the question that had been on his mind since the estate attorney had handed over the bad news.

"Greta," he began, "you knew about the sale and never told me?"

His question was met with a heavy sigh. "Rhett, how did you forget? The family land is what paid for Mom's final round of treatment."

A chill crawled up his spine and he squeezed his eyes shut. He did not want to talk about his mom. Especially her cancer. Rhett shook his head. "I don't remember agreeing to that."

Greta pushed on patiently. "Remember, Rhett? Dad was on the phone with the guy in Hickory Grove. They went through the last of their estate. Well, you weren't there. You were at the hospital. But we told you about it. They put the lot up for sale at a really low price hoping to have it sold in time to tell Mom that she didn't have to worry."

"Did it sell in time?" Rhett was wracking his brain but for the life of him could *not* recall *any* of what his sister was explaining.

"No, but it was close. I think that realtor, Mr. Hart, put an offer in just around the time of Mom's funeral. We had

Peter handle everything. Dad simply signed the paperwork a few days later. I knew about it because I asked. Maybe you were too—"

"Yeah, I know," he replied, blowing air out of his mouth as he eased into a wobbly kitchen chair and wiped his face with his hand.

"I thought when you texted me that you were going to try and buy the land back," his sister said.

Rhett had wanted to surprise her. He wanted to assess the property, make a plan—maybe even call in contractors—and then bring Greta down to Hickory Grove the day they broke ground and announce to her that half the acreage was hers. They could be neighbors, and she could build her dream house maybe.

The idea was possible only because of Rhett. His savings from flipping houses would set Greta and him up for life. And his little sister could use that. She was a teacher, and her pay was dang near minimum wage.

"No, I was going to build on Mom and Dad's land," Rhett answered, a deep sadness welling in his chest. He was disappointed in himself. Embarrassed, too. Had he really blocked out such crucial information? Was he really so distracted all those years?

Greta clicked her tongue like a mother hen. "Rhett, it's okay. And by the way, why would you want to move back to Hickory Grove? Emma hates small towns. And you have all those rentals in Louisville. I'd just as soon visit you in the city, besides."

"I'm *done* with the city, Greta. I never loved Louisville. I'm ready to go back home. You know?"

His sister sniffed. "Well what about Emma? Did you ever even ask her what she wanted?"

"We broke up. I'm staying in one of my units by the U." He didn't add that they'd broken up *after* his grand plans to relocate. What he also didn't say was that he didn't really care what Emma thought. He'd have moved to Hickory Grove without her if it ever came to that. Which it didn't.

"Oh," Greta replied, emotion gone from her voice. He always suspected Greta didn't exactly love his live-in girlfriend, but sometimes he wondered if it was simply because she was a live-in girlfriend and not a wife. Greta was traditional and preferred to refer to any of her own dates as male suitors and her situation as "*trying*" thanks to "a fast culture." He'd always laugh at that. His sweet little sister and her old-world ways.

"So what are you going to do now?" she asked.

"I'm not sure," Rhett replied, leaning forward and picking at a black scuff on the tabletop. "What would you do, Greta?"

"I never wanted to move back to Hickory Grove," she began. Rhett's heart sank a little. His head spun. It was a fool's mission all along, and he *knew* it. He just wouldn't accept it. "Why did *you* even want to go there, Rhett?"

He felt himself grow defensive. He was doing all of it for his little sister. So she could have something more than her crummy teacher apartment. So they both could have a nice home... a piece of Mom and Dad. But his sister didn't even want any of it. She had moved on. Gotten over their parents' death. He could not, for the life of him, imagine why. The last time they spoke—nearly a month or so ago now, well before he hatched his plan to see about the land—she had been on the same page as him. Vaguely discontent and searching. He had heard it in her voice. Her students were wearing her down. She was tired of living in her apartment complex. They were on the same page. It was the whole reason Rhett started brainstorming. It was the whole reason he started seeing his superficial relationship with Emma for what it was. It was the whole reason he made his plan.

Then he recalled. "Hey, Greta," he started, sitting up straight in his chair. "That Christmas cruise..."

Greta scheduled a Christmas cruise for herself and her girlfriends. Rhett was bummed they wouldn't be together to celebrate the holidays, but at the *time*, he had Emma and her oversized family to keep him occupied. All he remembered was getting a text from Greta when she returned home. It assured him that she was alive, and he distinctly remembered her gushing that it was the best time of her life.

"Yeah?" Greta asked coyly before a muffled voice rose in the background. She giggled.

His sister *giggled*. Like a teenager. "Greta Louisa Houston," Rhett scolded lightly. "Whose voice is that?"

Her giggle turned to laughter and she hissed something to the voice before answering her brother gleefully. "Rhett, I met someone."

And, with that, Rhett knew he had to let go of Hickory Grove.

He had to let go of his pain over his parents' deaths, and he had to let go of any lofty pipe dream about reuniting with Greta and making a go of recreating their childhood closeness.

It was time for Rhett to move on from his past. For once and for all.

Chapter 26 — Maggie

It had been twelve days of high tensions and nonstop packing and sorting and moving.

Becky, Fern, Theo, Zack and even Fern's husband, Stedman, had all chipped in to transfer everything that belonged to Maggie and her kids over to the farmhouse on County Road 131.

Through the stress, Maggie took great comfort in the fact that her friends—her *community*—had risen to the challenge and supported her. A meal train, courtesy of town busybody Liesl Hart, was in motion for Maggie's first full week in the farmhouse. That week would start the following Monday, but Maggie figured it would be smart to begin staying in the farmhouse while they still had claim to their old place. Just in case they realized they'd forgotten something or wanted to go back *just one more time*.

In fact, they hadn't forgotten anything. The house on Pine Tree Lane was cleared and ready for bank possession, as depressing as that sounded. Her neighbor Fern, at one point, threatened to push all her junk out onto the driveway and front yard in order to bring down property values just to spite "the powers that be," as she'd said. But Maggie reminded everyone that the real villain was Travis, not the people in Hickory Grove who did their jobs.

It was early afternoon, and the boys were still at school; Gretchen had taken Briar to go on their first (though modest—necessities only!) grocery trip for the farmhouse, which is a thing Maggie would have been excited to do were it not for the insurmountable task of the day: to make the place livable for a night. Becky had to drive to Corydon for work. Fern was working.

It amazed Maggie how fast life picked up and moved on. Not that she needed anyone, but still.

Theo was up at Notre Dame for the start of his spring classes, but it seemed that he'd be returning for the weekend and spending much of it with Gretchen, if her constant texting was any indication.

Then again, by that logic, Rhett Houston would be returning for the weekend, too. But Maggie knew he wasn't. He told her about setting himself up in one of his tenants' studios after some college kid broke his lease agreement. It was fate, Rhett had said.

Fate.

Fate that he go back to Louisville and stay there, probably. *C'est la vie*, as Marguerite would have said.

And so, it was just Maggie there on County Road 131, alone for an hour in a creaking house in the middle of the woods far, far from any place she'd ever known. Alone, save for the distinct feeling that she was *not* alone. Perhaps that was a typical thing with old houses handed down through the generations. Someone was there with her.

Maybe her mom.

Maggie felt a sob form in her throat. Sadness and anxiety weren't often a part of the redhead's world. She was continually surrounded by people. Noisy, happy people.

Even though Hickory Grove was too small for a downtown—or an uptown—and its central hub was nothing more than the crossroads of Main Street and Overlook Lane, Maggie had always lived her life right there: in the heart of it all. She'd never had cause to be alone, and she had never been so alone.

Earlier in the week, Zack had helped her handle the divorce paperwork, but they were still waiting on Travis to sign so they could file. The deal Maggie offered was clear. Full custody would go to her, but he could see the kids whenever he wanted as long as he gave due notice. He could request them for a weekend so long as he could prove he had a place for the children to sleep safely. Alternatively, the children could stay at Travis's mother's house for a weekend. All this had to be on the up-and-up, but it was an option for him. No child support required.

And though Travis had made two gravely poor choices of late—allowing their mortgage to default and taking off like a scared weasel when times got tough, Maggie still cared about him. Even if he was with some other woman, he was still the father of her children.

But never again would he be Maggie's husband.

In some ways, she liked to think, he never really was.

Thoughts of Rhett flit in and out of her mind as she got to work in the parlor. After he left, she just could not shake the thought of him. But it didn't bother her. Rather, it was the other thing—other than the drifting non-memories of her ancestors who'd lived in that very house—that kept her company as she got down to work.

Maggie's plan, then, was to deep clean one room at a time. They could all camp out in the parlor the first night. They had the mattresses leaning against the foyer and front hall walls, ready for business.

Vacuuming the floors was hard enough what with years and years of dust and dirt and whatever else had ground into the cracks and crevices, but once she began on the decades-old sofas, she realized some of what her family had left there was simply not salvageable.

Maggie finished vacuuming, dumped the can of her upright and set about a second round, then a third, then rolled the vacuum out and swapped in her mop and bucket.

In the days before they finished moving everything, Fern helped her see about getting hot water running. In all, they had to have the septic pumped, the well tested, and the water person ensure the pump was set up and working, and then reestablish electricity. Maggie found herself surprised that her grandparents ever even had electricity running to the out-of-the-way property. It had to have been an expensive upgrade.

But the place was as well maintained as could be, thanks in large part to old Marguerite.

So, Maggie had running water and basic electricity. However, she did not have *hot* water or the use of any appliances. And, most bizarrely, she did not have a toilet.

They planned to shower at Becky's house, but Maggie quickly realized that cleaning without hot water was difficult at best. She paid for the septic out of her cash hoard. She paid for the well assessment and service. She found out that Dirk had been paying taxes on the property for the past few months, but surely she'd need to take over on that. Plus, she had to put up money to file for divorce just as soon as Travis got around to signing.

Maggie was officially low on money. She had no access to her credit card or ability to get a new one. And she hadn't done hair in over a week.

So, a water heater and a toilet had officially become luxury items.

Taking a deep breath, she reminded herself just one room at a time. They had a place to shower. They could continue with dry food or takeout for a few days more—until they got the fridge going or the meal train began. She just needed to line up some clients. Maybe start looking into a night shift at Mally's or something.

And though Maggie hated to ask Gretchen to help financially, it was a back-up plan. If things got dire, Gretchen could help. Would help. She was a good girl. Maggie's children were good children.

An hour later, Maggie had effectively scrubbed the wooden floor of the parlor into submission, and only once did she wish it was covered in linoleum like the halls and kitchen.

Gretchen and Briar had returned with a modest haul which served to remind Maggie to once again tackle the daunting task of prying open the old Frigidaire. It couldn't have been in that bad of shape, based on its exterior.

"I think it's very cool that we have an antique fridge," Gretchen offered, as she neatly organized the five paper sacks on the kitchen table.

Maggie nodded. "It'd be cooler if we could crack it open."

Maggie now wondered if she ought to have taken Fern up on her suggestion to take their old fridge and move it to the farmhouse. However, Maggie worried over asking her generous helpers to lift and haul one more thing. "Besides," she had answered, "we have a fridge at the farmhouse."

Now, as the two women tried with all their might to tug loose the white door, Maggie could kick herself.

"We can always go back and get ours if this one won't open or if it doesn't work, like Miss Fern said," Maggie told Gretchen as she scooted the unit forward from the wall to assess the back of it. A humming noise purred and air blew up from a vent at the bottom. So, by all accounts, it was operable. And she *really* didn't want to go back to the Pine Tree house unless she absolutely *had* to. Besides, her fridge there wasn't anything to write home about. It was probably almost as old as the farmhouse one.

"I've got an idea. Let's see if there's a crowbar in that barn out back," Gretchen suggested.

Maggie scooped Briar into her arms and out they went, through the weedy path toward what once must have been a thing of beauty. The red paint had long begun to fade and peel, but the old barn was broad and sturdy-looking.

It was filled with possibilities.

As though Gretchen were reading her mother's mind, she said, "Mom, we could *do* something with this." She waved her hand out across the front.

"Yeah, Gretch. Rent it out maybe? Get a little income going."

Gretchen peered at Maggie out of the corner of her eye. "I could set up my crafting station in here. I really could start learning to sew! Who knows, maybe Marguerite or Mimi De-vereux left behind an old Singer." The teenager glowed with ex-citement, and Maggie knew better than to quell it.

They arrived at the doors to learn the boys had been right. A sturdy chain hung down from the latch, rust obscuring its level of effectiveness. An old padlock dragged the chain low. Maggie set Briar down and lifted the padlock, latent red dust smudging onto her skin as she pulled with all her might.

"Do you have a key?" Gretchen asked.

Maggie shook her head. "I tried all the keys the other day. None worked."

"Hmm, well..." Gretchen glanced around, searching for something.

"Did we bring any of Daddy's tools from the shed?" Maggie asked her daughter, feeling the pull of exhaustion blur her memory.

Gretchen shrugged. "I don't know. I thought we brought everything."

"Let's check. Maybe Zack or Stedman hauled it over."

The women rounded back to the side of the house, where boxes marked *Exterior* sat waiting, ready to rot into the earth.

After rummaging through every last one, they came up empty.

"The milk is going to spoil," Gretchen pointed out.

Maggie sighed. "That's not helpful. Maybe you should take the groceries to the Pine Tree house for now. I'll keep looking for a key or a crowbar, okay?"

"What about Briar?" Gretchen gestured to the little girl who had since wandered back toward the barn, collecting as many weeds as she could in her grubby little hands.

"I'll watch her. You go. We can't afford to waste so much as a dozen eggs." Maggie hadn't intended on transferring her stress to her daughter, but it was best Gretchen realize the gravity of their situation now. Maggie added, "Oh, Gretch. It's after three. Can you pick up the boys, too?"

Gretchen nodded and packed the bags back into the SUV without complaining and peeled away from the house and up the dirt road back to town.

And then Maggie's phone rang.

"THIS IS A WILD QUESTION, and I *know* that," came the voice on the other end. It was Becky, who was driving back from Corydon as she spoke.

Maggie strode back to the house where she could start setting up mattresses with sheets and blankets, Briar whining behind her about being cold.

Fortunately the parlor had a fireplace and every last one of Maggie's space heaters was running on full blast, but still the place felt chilly.

"I like wild questions," Maggie answered, directing Briar to a snack at the kitchen table and wrapping her in an extra towel she hadn't yet employed in her mission to deep clean every last corner.

Becky went on, "Didn't you used to own chickens? Like... hens or something?"

"Wait, what?" Maggie wasn't certain she heard Becky right. "Well, yes. But, why?"

"Maggie, I bought a darn chicken. It was an impulse purchase. I don't know what I was thinking except the idea of having fresh eggs was super enticing and—-"

"Becky, a *chicken*? Who is selling chickens in January in Indiana? Is it just one? Not a chick but a full-grown chicken? Like a hen?"

"Yeah, Maggie, listen, they were rehoming her and a few others, and she was dirt cheap, and I thought Memaw still had her old coop..."

"But..." Maggie prompted her friend, seeing clearly where this could be going, and it was almost maddening.

"Well Memaw doesn't have a coop anymore. We looked everywhere, and she's mad at me. But I did notice the other day that your farmhouse has one, so..."

"So you want to board your single chicken here, in the middle of my catastrophe?" Maggie should have been annoyed. She should have been angry, even, that her friend was completely deaf to all of Maggie's problems at that moment and wanted to unload yet another problem on her.

"No, no, no," Becky replied. "I just need the coop, that's all."

Maggie blew out a sigh and told her to come on over. "And bring the chicken with you."

"ANY WORD FROM TRAVIS?" It was the first thing to slip out of Becky's mouth, despite the fact that she had a restless, wild-eyed hen locked up in a cage in the bed of her truck in the dead of winter.

Maggie shook her head, "Not a peep. Zack said he has a certain timeline to respond before other things happen, but frankly I don't even care. I need to get this place in decent shape. Whatever else happens is just noise."

"Like the hen," Becky answered, amusement filling her face.

Maggie cracked a smile. "My disaster is not a *joke*, Becky," she tsked. "Now that poor chicken must be freezing. You're going to need more than a century-old chicken outdoor coop, you know."

"No, I don't know. But it sounds like you do."

"Yes. We had chickens on Pine Tree Lane. Years ago. When I was still young and deluded that my life was perfect."

Becky frowned. "Aw, Mags," she began as they huddled together in the cold.

A single tear welled along Maggie's lower eyelid, dancing there for a moment until the breeze cut in through the trees and whisked it off the rim of her lashes and smeared it into the bridge of her nose. Maggie wiped the wetness with the back of her hand, thankful it was a renegade and the floodgates were still securely in place.

That was the benefit of hard labor; it kept you from falling in on yourself.

But then Becky took her by surprise and grabbed her in a hard hug, threatening Maggie's emotional state yet again. Her friend whispered into Maggie's ear, "Just because it doesn't seem perfect *now*, doesn't mean you didn't have happy times."

Maggie nodded her head and forced herself to concentrate on the tasks in her mental to-do list: a sleeping room, functioning fridge, hot water. Those were the priorities. In that order.

Following up on Travis was useless and would result in nothing but stress.

Maggie squeezed her friend back, thankful for the perspective she brought and the silliness of her visit. "Let's see the darn thing. I think this could be a good distraction for me," she announced.

Becky hefted a small wire cage from the bed of the truck. Inside, a panicked chicken bobbed its head about.

"I can't believe you did this. Is Memaw like *super* mad?"

Becky was living with her grandmother on the Linden family farm off of Main Street. She'd probably stay there until sweet Memaw passed on. Becky, like Fern, loved old things. Maggie often wondered why they hadn't formed a tighter bond. Then again, perhaps they had and Maggie was too consumed to realize it. A stupid adolescent jealousy might have taken root in Maggie's heart over Fern and Becky and their potential for closeness. But she was too exhausted to care or be bothered over such trivialities.

"Memaw is not happy about it. She made me feel five-years-old all over again and said I'd better figure something out because she wasn't lifting a finger, period. She said she'd done her fair share of chicken rearing and for far too long. Her chicken days are over, I guess."

"You have no coop, you have an unsupportive roommate, it's the dead of winter, and your best friend in the world is going through pure hell. And you bought a chicken."

"She's a hen, remember," Becky pointed out sheepishly. "But, I can take her back. You're right. It's like I'm going through a midlife crisis. I don't know. Zack won't be happy, either; I can assure you of that."

"Oh great, Beck." Just then the SUV came blowing up the dirt drive. Once Gretchen parked, the kids poured out like jelly from an overstuffed PB&J sandwich. Briar, who'd been inside, intuited the excitement and tumbled down the front deck, on the precipice of crying but too determined to be part of the big kids' discovery to care that she scraped her knee.

"Is that a chicken?" Ky hollered, sprinting full speed in his puffy winter jacket. Dakota and Briar rushed in, too.

Gretchen, heavy-lidded and irritable, said, "I went to drop the groceries at our house."

"Thanks, Gretchen," Maggie began to answer but the teenager interrupted.

"I couldn't, though." Her face was serious. As she grew nearer, Maggie realized she wasn't irritated or tired.

The hollow look in her eyes didn't reveal the stress and exhaustion present in each of them, at that moment.

No.

She was frightened.

"Gretchen, what is it? What happened?"

The kids fell silent. Becky grew still. Even the chicken stopped rustling in her cage.

"Mom, when I went to the house," she began, her eyes darting from the kids to Becky and back to Maggie. "Dad was there."

Chapter 27 — Gretchen

Gretchen was not afraid of her father. But she knew better than to trust him. So she'd booked it, sacrificing fresh milk in favor of maintaining her dignity. Because if she had jumped out of the SUV to confront him, she knew it would end in an all-out sob fest with her dad winning on the basis of his indifference and her losing because she cared.

A lot.

Though Gretchen loved the new farmhouse and all its potential, she hated who her father was and the position he'd put them in. And she hated him for more reasons than that. She hated him because he was a loser who'd rather hit the bar than read a book to his kids, and mostly, because he left them. Without a fight and without a reason. He just left.

What kind of father did that to his children? To his wife?

Then Gretchen remembered that her grandfather had done that. Years ago. Not just her father's father, but her mother's father too.

Gretchen came from a long line of men who left their families.

And that sucked.

So it was curious that she called Theo.

Their exchange was brief, because she didn't want Dakota or Ky to hear her conversation, but Theo promised he'd come down Friday night. He'd help. He'd be there for her. At least, that was how the conversation began.

But then, to Gretchen's own surprise, she'd told him no.

It took every bit of intellectual maturity and wisdom she had to realize that she did not *need* Theo to fix the problem of her dad. And, even more importantly, she did not *want* him to.

What she needed—*and* wanted—was to have someone to talk to. That was it. A friend. A confidant. A venting partner. She didn't want romance or pillow talk or acts of bravery.

Tragically, Theo did not want to hear that.

Because when Gretchen told him that she didn't *need him to save her* and that she just wanted to talk to a friend, he replied in the most disappointing way she could imagine.

He said he was sick of her wishy-washiness. He said that *he was* her friend.

But he also said that he wanted to be more.

And for Gretchen, the revelation was ruinous.

Chapter 28 — Maggie

Becky slammed a hand down on the wood. "He told you *what*?"

The three women were sitting at the breakfast table in the kitchen. The boys and Briar had been assigned to set up the chicken coop, and Maggie didn't even care if they were dragging her good duvet out there as bedding.

Gretchen's news was urgent.

"Forget about Theo for a second," Maggie cut in. "Let's start with Travis."

Poor Gretchen had borne the brunt of not only running into her derelict father but also of dealing with a teenaged boy who didn't know quite how to handle grown-up problems, yet. Unfortunately, Gretchen failed to realize Theo had good intentions. And, she also failed to realize that Theo was a catch. She was too absorbed in her own struggles to see that or to understand that people make mistakes.

But those mistakes don't always have to be an ending.

Still, Theo and his untimely comment were, frankly, secondary to the matter of Travis.

Becky apologized and agreed. "Yes, you're right. Sorry."

Maggie punched into the pop top of a Diet Coke and sipped slowly, the cool beverage coating her throat and giving her enough energy to screw her courage to the sticking place.

"Gretchen, spill. What did he look like? Did he talk do you? Was he trying to move back in or something? Was he looking for his stuff?"

After a deep inhale, the teenager offered all the details she could. "He looked tired. He had a scruffy face and his hair was growing in." Gretchen gestured to the sides of her head like she was emulating a mad scientist.

Travis had grown bald on top in his twenties, and ever since Maggie had pointed it out, he'd never skipped a day shaving. He'd fully embraced the bald-headed look as long as he was in control of it.

"Like on top?" Becky asked, her eyes wide as though the biggest chunk of gossip to come from all this drama was that Travis, suddenly, had hair.

Maggie chuckled in spite of herself. "Maybe he had the hairs from his hairy behind tweezed out and transplanted to the top of his head."

Gretchen, who'd previously been on the brink of sobbing, scrunched her face in disgust. "Eww, Mom. Come *on*. And it was just on the sides, anyway. He looked really, well, *old*."

Becky broke out in a full-blown belly laugh, and Maggie ignored her daughter to join in.

"Maybe it's a toupee!" Becky added, as Maggie roared along with her.

She threw in one last joke through the tears of laughter that streaked down her cheeks. "A toupee for a butthead!"

It felt good. And though Maggie had always been careful never to criticize her husband to her children or in front of them, a little fun-poking had its place in light of recent events.

Even Gretchen cracked a grin before waving her hands to continue the narrative. "*Anyway*," she said, smiling still, "he mostly looked confused, honestly. He had a big box on the front porch and was talking on his cell phone."

"Ah, so it *works* still," Maggie jumped in. "He really is just ignoring us."

"But that was all I saw before I drove off," Gretchen concluded.

Becky asked, "Did he see you?"

Gretchen shook her head. "I don't know. I don't know how he could have missed the SUV, but I didn't stop to check. I just sped out of there. Sorry about the food, Mom."

"What food?" Becky asked.

"She was going to take the groceries to our fridge at the old house. But, it's so cold out, Gretch, I'm sure they'll be fine in the SUV. Probably even better there anyway. And Becky's here, now. Maybe she can take the meat and dairy back to her place in a while."

"Well, sure, but what is wrong with the fridge here?"

"Sealed shut. We probably need to get a new one or try to bring the one from Pine Tree down here."

Becky nodded. "I can take your food to my place. In fact, how about you all come on over. Memaw is making fried pork chops. I'll have her throw a couple extra in the skillet. You can shower up and sleep warm."

Maggie had to admit a hot shower and southern cooking sounded amazing. So she agreed readily, after nearly two weeks of brushing off her friend's offers of a refuge. "But what about the chicken?"

"Let's go check," Becky suggested. And the three rose from the table and descended from the back door toward the two boys and little Briar, who had made far more progress than Maggie would have expected.

The coop was decrepit, but they'd added blankets and a water dish.

"This place is starting to actually seem like a real farm," Becky murmured, apparently in awe of the plentiful, ragamuffin children and their new pet livestock. Maggie smiled at the sight.

"What's the temp dropping to tonight?" Gretchen pulled out her phone. "Ugh," she said, opening her text messaging app instead and flashing it to Maggie and Becky who gawked on in great interest over the teenage love drama.

Maggie's eyes scanned Theo's latest message. It was sweet. Sincere. An apology. Sort of. "Gretch," she began, looking to Becky for some sort of approval.

Becky's mouth drew down in a pout. She met Maggie's gaze and nodded before saying, "Gretchen, I don't want to get in the middle here, but Theo just likes you. A lot. He can't tell if you like him back, and that's hard. You know?"

Gretchen smirked and swiped around on her phone. "It's going to be 38 for a low. The chicken might be okay. We can research more at Miss Becky's house, you all," she called to her younger siblings.

Maggie saw through her daughter's act, though. "Gretchen, did you hear what Becky said to you?"

The boys and Briar ambled off toward the SUV, Becky trailing behind slowly enough to stay part of Maggie and Gretchen's conversation.

"Yeah, I heard you, Miss Becky." Gretchen's voice dropped lower. "And I like Theo, too. But I don't need him to 'save' me," she spat, quoting the air with her fingers.

Nodding, Maggie answered, "You don't want to be like me, do you?"

Gretchen turned, taken aback at her mother's perceptiveness. "That's not..."

"It is what you're thinking, and that's good, sweetheart." Maggie slipped her hand around her daughter's waist. She felt thin, too thin. "Gretchen, there are good things about your dad. He provided for us very well for a very long time, you know."

"Provided for us? He's the reason we're *here*." The girl passed her hand out across the colorless, barren property.

Maggie sighed. "He's half the reason, Gretchen. But I'm the other half."

She frowned at her mother. "What do you mean? *He* did this to us. He's always been a loser."

"Gretchen, I didn't stand up for myself. Or for you all. I didn't put my foot down when I should have. I didn't ask questions when I should have. If I had, things would be different. I take half the blame. I know it's not my fault Travis was a drinker or didn't really know how to be a good father. But it was my choice to marry him and have kids with him. And it was my choice to stick around. But you know what, Gretch? It wasn't all bad. After all, some good came from it."

"Like what?" Gretchen asked.

A laugh escaped Maggie's mouth. "Like you kids, for starters."

Gretchen smiled and turned to hug her mom.

The others were in the car waiting, but Maggie felt compelled to add one more thing. "I know you want to make better choices than I did, Gretchen. But don't forget to live your life a little, too, okay? God's grace is here. With us. All the time."

Her daughter nodded solemnly.

"And one more thing, Gretch." Maggie pulled the young girl closer to whisper into her ear, "Dating Theo wouldn't be such a bad choice."

Chapter 29 — Rhett

He was lost.

Rhett had never been lost in his entire life. Not as a child and certainly not as an adult. But he was standing there, locked into a grid of towering skyscrapers as people whisked this way and that.

Having no clue which way was north or even what city he was in, Rhett tried to approach a woman waiting by the broad glassy wall behind them.

"Excuse me, ma'am," he began, but she recoiled.

Nervous now, Rhett glanced down to see he was wearing jeans and a t-shirt. Nothing seemed off.

He left the woman and started walking up the street to a crosswalk only to realize it was an illusion.

The sidewalk and the street parallel to it faded off into a massive painting of a cityscape.

Rhett turned, and behind him, the scene played on as usual. People waving for taxi cabs and staring at their phones. People climbing into rideshares. People disappearing into the glass walled buildings. People frowning.

A man stood texting on the corner next to him, and Rhett tried once again to make sense of it all.

"Hey man, can you tell me—-"

"Go home, kid," the business-suit-clad jerk huffed dryly and turned on his heel back toward a building.

A buzzing sound thrummed into Rhett's brain, and he woke with a start.

It was a dream.

He inhaled sharply and rubbed his face with his hands. Adding to the confusion, his new dog stirred to life and hobbled over, clamping his left front paw on the mattress and panting hot milk bone breath on Rhett's face.

He figured that if he was going to live the bachelor life in a studio by the University of Louisville, then he ought to do it right.

So just the day before, he went to the local rescue and picked out the oldest, saddest looking dog there.

The pooch's keepers said the poor guy had been wandering downtown before someone collected him and dropped him off. With no name tag or microchip, the rescue decided to call him Old Gray.

Rhett liked that. And he sort of liked the dog's beginnings, too.

Old Gray probably wasn't good for much more than companionship, but that was all Rhett needed.

He snatched his phone from the far side of his lumpy pillow and squinted at the bright screen. A text from Greta.

She was going to be in Corydon later and would love to meet up. Her new boyfriend was with her, too.

Rhett groaned and eyed Old Gray who let out a wet sneeze.

"My sentiments exactly, Boy." But, technically, this *was* what Rhett had wanted. To reconnect with his sister. Have something more in life than work and a lousy girlfriend.

After replying that he would be there, Rhett got out of bed and got dressed.

THE INTRODUCTION HAD gone fine enough. Greta's boyfriend, Kadan, was a nice city boy. He worked "in Tech," which made Rhett want to chuckle, but he didn't dare. He had a sinking feeling that anyone who worked "in Tech" took himself a little seriously.

Even so, Greta was clearly enamored, and their relationship appeared stable. Besides, Kadan was obviously a good—albeit uptight—guy. A good person. And that was the bottom line for Rhett.

Even good people worked "in Tech." Just because Rhett preferred plumbing to programming, it didn't mean that Kadan wouldn't take care of Greta.

They'd left on a positive note, and Rhett was then free to head back to Louisville. Old Gray had camped out happily in the cab of his truck for the duration of the luncheon, and now, as Rhett climbed in behind the steering wheel, he felt overwhelming waves of emotion sweep through him.

Old Gray took notice and rested his head on Rhett's thigh, just as happy to get a scrub down as Rhett was to give it.

"Where to now, Boy?" Rhett whispered, considering his options.

Each of his rentals was—knock on wood—fine. No tenant complaints. No upcoming turnovers to make.

His house search, however, was abysmal.

Rhett had made a clear list of non-negotiables. Three bedrooms, two baths. Over an acre—he had to make up for losing the family land. And, finally, outside of the city. Even just by a mile. No way did he want to be trapped in the grid. Period.

His price point was flexible, but that didn't seem to help. Anyone who had a house that met his criteria was apparently happy enough to keep it.

Rhett cut the wheel back onto County Road 40 and into Hickory Grove, making his way toward Main Street, where he would turn onto Highway 211.

But as he pulled up to a stop at the four way, a black low-rider turned in front of him.

Driving it: none other than Travis Engel.

A FEELING OF UNEASE crept over Rhett and he grabbed his phone to call Maggie.

It rang until her voicemail picked up. A cheery greeting befitting of a happy homemaking hairdresser. It didn't quite sound like the girl he'd known in high school.

He tried again only to meet the same result.

A car pulled up behind him, so instead of turning left back toward Louisville, he drove forward and veered off to the right, parking in front of the bank as he kept his eye on Travis's slow-moving vehicle.

Rhett first expected him to turn into the garage, but when the low-rider buzzed past that, Rhett wondered if he'd turn directly onto Pine Tree Lane. Again, Travis kept driving.

Squarely in the direction of County Road 131.

After a failed effort of finding Becky's or Fern's phone numbers in his device, and realizing he had no way to get ahold of Maggie other than her own line, he made a decision.

And followed Travis.

RHETT HAD LEFT NO FEWER than five voicemails and the same number of texts before committing to what felt increasingly like a vigilante mission.

Old Gray was now sitting at alert and focused in the passenger seat, and Rhett took that to mean that either the dog trusted Rhett's decision and was equally committed, or that the dog, like Rhett, sensed something bad was going to happen.

Either way, Rhett knew he could not live with himself if Travis wound up at the farm and something happened to Maggie or the kids.

And while Rhett wasn't convinced that Travis was coward enough to actually hurt a woman or a child, he still didn't trust the guy.

Chapter 30 — Maggie

I t was Saturday.

Maggie usually did hair on Saturdays—all day, too. Unfortunately or fortunately, she had no clients lined up for that day. But she promised herself she would get bookings going for the following week.

Gretchen was working the early shift at Mally's with plans to study with a friend after she got off. Her practicum was the next week, and it was crucial.

Theo had come to town and had offered to help Maggie until Gretchen got home, but Maggie had the boys for that. Apparently, Gretchen had listened to Maggie after all. Otherwise, Theo was simply dead set on making something happen. Maggie wasn't sure which.

For the full morning, Becky was watching Briar.

Theo, the day before, had brought over his tools with the goal to unstick the fridge. He, too, figured maybe the gasket had melted a little and glued the thing shut.

In fact, Fern, who'd visited the day before as well, guessed it was a stuck latch. And she was right. The antique fridge had a latching door rather than a magnetic one, and though Maggie jimmied the handle, she hadn't thought about the latch.

Luckily, to his credit, Becky's son was refreshingly handy, popping the latch out with a screwdriver. From there, she intended to soak it in vinegar to clear the rust before she brought Theo back to re-attach it. But Fern warned her otherwise, reminding her, "*Those old fridges kill kids, Maggie! Upgrade NOW.*"

"Ky!" she hollered out the front door, which the boys had left open on their way from the second floor outside to the wood stack.

They'd just finished the third bedroom upstairs and their progress was becoming more pronounced. The biggest obstacle was having to go to the bathroom in the woods, but Maggie found it wasn't too terrible an interruption. There *was* proper plumbing for a toilet but it had been removed and covered with an early model space heater. For whatever reason.

It wasn't the only odd remnant of the late seventies. Upon one of Maggie's many walk-throughs, she'd encountered antiques that would make Fern drool, heirlooms that she'd never known about, and oddities that spun more questions than they answered.

It all reminded Maggie that she and her brother had history. It was there, living in that farmhouse. She just had to uncover it.

And maybe, just maybe, she'd discover more than a broken, old toilet hidden somewhere on the property.

Sighing in the doorframe to the kitchen, she took it all in. The porcelain farmhouse sink with what had to be original plumbing.

The death-trap fridge.

The turn-of-the-century (*if even that modern?*) wood-burning stove, complete with a little slot for an oven.

Whatever had become of the family who lived there? *Her* family? Her very own mother, the tragedy of it all. The center of it, too?

Maggie's eyes moved back to the sink. It would be her starting point.

She set about filling a stock pot with water then transferred it to the stove.

"Ky! Dakota!" she called again. "Where's the wood for the stove?"

When neither boy replied, Maggie draped her yellow rubber gloves over the apron of the sink and strode through the parlor to the front door, which stood open.

A frigid wind struck her in the face, and she quickly stepped out of the door and closed it behind her before lifting her eyes to scan the property for her sons.

But she didn't have to. They were standing right there, at the foot of the porch steps, facing a black truck and a man leaning against it, grinning from ear to ear.

Travis.

"I DIDN'T KNOW YOU HAD an inheritance, Maggie. Jeez, girl, we could have used this old dump to help with the bills." Travis pushed off from the truck with his hands in his pockets, a lazy sneer painted across his scruffy face.

"Boys, get in the house," Maggie directed, moving down the stairs and shuffling them up behind her.

"Hey, those are my kids, too, you know." He hocked a glob of phlegm, shooting it like biological warfare at the dead wildflowers to the left of the porch.

Maggie took a deep breath. "Why'd you leave, Travis? Why didn't you tell me you weren't paying the mortgage?"

"I guess," he answered immediately, "because I got sick of everything. Paying the bills. Working full-time—back-breaking labor, mind you. That, and..."

"Another woman?"

Travis's smile fell away. "I'd never cheat on you, Maggie. But temptation was there. I can admit that now." He kept silent a moment, until the temporal shadow on his face lifted.

His eyes were tired and sad. And, though Maggie didn't quite see the boy she once knew—that handsome teenage bad boy with a muscle car and tattoo... the one who made her feel *alive* when the world around her was so decrepit... the one who promised to take her from that apartment with stifling Great Aunt Marguerite and show her what happiness could be and how much fun they could have—well, she saw *something*.

That Travis was not evil. A villain, maybe. But not evil.

"Travis," she began, meeting his gaze at last. "Did you sign the papers?"

He held up a finger and reached into his passenger window. "These papers? Divorce? Custody? Blah, blah, blah?"

Maggie nodded, turning nervous again.

Shaking his head, he dug a lighter out of his front pocket. "I'm not giving you up, Maggie. I made a mistake, sure, but I am not a quitter. You hear that?"

She swallowed as he held a small flame at the bottom corner of that fresh white stack. The stack that had been sitting on her former kitchen table not two weeks before.

In one sense, everything had changed since that moment. But in another, nothing had. It was all simply coming to a head.

She wondered where this would go. Should she call the police? Or Becky? Would Travis leave?

Maggie rolled her shoulders back and down and took another step toward Travis, her hands open at her waist. "Why are you here, Travis?"

The packet had finally caught fire and once the flames had eaten half of it, Travis dropped the silly show to the frostbitten ground, leaving it to silently sizzle. Maggie stared at the half-charred rubbish and felt sad for the man standing before her.

She took another step toward him. "Have you talked to your mom?" she pressed, trying any angle to soften the situation.

He licked his lips and returned her gaze, his eyes narrowing. "Maggie, I won't leave you again. I won't leave the kids. I'll be better. I'll *do* better." His voice shook with the promises, and as Maggie took one more step closer she could smell it on his breath.

Putrid and familiar—the smell of stale beer. Maybe not much, but enough for the cold January wind to hurtle it into Maggie's face, spurring a stark realization.

If it weren't for his driving drunk, Travis was not a danger to anyone but himself.

She knew she needed to call the police. Because she was done exposing her children to such a mess.

"Travis, we can talk about a custody arrangement another time. In the meantime. You need to leave. I'll have new paperwork mailed to you; it'll be fine, okay?" She searched his eyes for an answer, but his gaze was now on the house behind her.

Her hand trembling, Maggie reached for her phone in her back pocket.

But it wasn't there. She'd left it upstairs earlier. She could picture the stupid thing, sitting on the floor in the corner of the front bedroom.

Maggie knew that Travis wouldn't hurt her. Or any of the kids. But he was under the influence and clearly committed to some sort of reunion.

Helplessness consumed Maggie until she heard the engine of a vehicle humming in the distance. She wondered if it was Becky, bringing Briar back. Or Fern, conducting a welfare check just because. She wondered if it was just an errant driver en route to western Indiana.

But Maggie also wondered when she was going to solve her own problems for once.

"I'm going to get my phone. Stay here, Travis." The words didn't feel like her own. Sharp and firm, they marked the strength of a soldier instead of the panic of a subdued and neglected wife.

Travis lunged half-heartedly after her and tripped on his own shoes before sliding on the heels of his palms down onto the icy dirt path.

Maggie left him there and dashed inside, locking the door behind herself as she met the worried faces of Dakota and Ky.

Anger rose up in her throat at the thought of them seeing this reality. But, relief followed soon after.

It was better they knew.

"Dakota, run up to the front bedroom and grab my phone," she directed calmly.

Ky, her sweet, innocent Ky, tugged on Maggie's arm. She looked down at him to see tears welling up in his eyes.

"It's okay, sweetheart," she whispered, bending and wrapping the child in her arms. "It's okay."

"Are you calling the police on him?" Ky squeaked through soft sobs.

Maggie hushed her little boy gently and rocked his body in her arms. "I'm calling his mother, Ky. Mamaw will help."

"But she's never helped us before," Dakota replied from midway down the staircase.

Maggie peeked out the window. Travis had righted himself, but he was faced away, staring off.

"Mothers help their children," Maggie answered her older son. "No matter what."

Ky squeezed Maggie tighter, Dakota skipped down the few steps until he, too, wedged himself into their hug.

Another glance outside revealed that Travis no longer stood swaying by his truck.

Nervous, Maggie gripped the phone and scrolled for her mother-in-law's number, hitting the call icon and commanding that the boys stay inside with the door locked.

Then, she stepped out.

The phone to her ear, ringing. Mamaw Engel answered immediately. In hushed tones Maggie conveyed the events as succinctly as possible.

And just as she hung up, she found him. Nearly one hundred yards off, by the main road. Through scraggly, winter-worn oaks and brush, she could barely make out who Travis was talking to.

But then she saw.

It was Rhett.

Her heart pounded in her chest, and Maggie broke out into a jog.

They saw her, and Travis's face fell into a deeper scowl.

"Since he won't answer," her husband began, sloppily hooking a thumb back toward Maggie's old friend, "why don't *you* tell me what in the world is going on?"

Maggie met Rhett's even gaze and found that she could solve this.

She always could.

But Maggie found something else, too. She found that she had never said exactly what she needed. Not to Travis. Not to Marguerite. Not to Rhett, either.

She'd always let things happen to her... or for her. It was never Maggie who drove her life, and for the simple reason that she never clearly *said anything*.

"Travis, we're done. I want a divorce, and I want you to leave. Now. And if you don't—" she flicked a glance to Rhett, who nodded to her solemnly. "If you don't leave, I'm calling the police."

Travis let out a low whistle. "I didn't realize we were doing threats now," he slurred.

Rhett took a step away from his truck and toward Travis, his eyes still on Maggie.

But she didn't falter or give in. And, she didn't care what Travis had to say, anyway, because she had the confidence of a freed woman.

Though... it didn't hurt to have broad-shouldered Rhett Houston waiting in the wings, ready to be her reinforcer. Her hero.

"It's not a threat, Travis. It's a promise."

The man stumbled forward, but Rhett grabbed the back of his denim jacket and with a quick jerk, Travis was on the ground, whimpering like a dog.

Maggie looked up, ensuring that the boys couldn't see them.

Then she realized it was okay.

It was okay if the boys saw this. Because all they *had* seen for all of their lives was Maggie acting like a doormat.

For once, it would be good for them to see a real man step up and help a woman.

And, it was good for them to see Maggie take control of the situation. She wanted those boys to see her as the strong woman... the type of woman she hoped they would respect. The type of woman she hoped they would one day marry.

"Travis, get up," she spat.

Rhett frowned at her, interrupting. "Maggie, I can drive him into town. Or we can go ahead and call the authorities. Tell me what you need from me. I'm here."

She smiled gratefully at him, wondering *why*, exactly, he was there, but knowing, of course, that she was happy to have him.

Despite her renewed gumption and despite her confidence, Maggie knew something else.

She wouldn't always be perfectly strong. She wouldn't always make the right choices.

But she *would* always have her friends.

And Maggie knew that no matter what pickle she got herself into, she could rely on the kindness of those good people in her life. Maggie could depend on her Hickory Grove community and her best friends.

Maybe especially the one who felt like he was a little more than a friend, after all.

Chapter 31 — Gretchen

S he was confused.

A text message came through to her phone from her mom. But it was Dakota, with a message of alarm.

And it made no sense. Why would their father show up at the farm when he was entirely MIA, for one. And secondly, how would he know about it? As far as everyone thought, Travis was in the dark on the inheritance.

How had he found out?

She wondered all this and more as she drove anxiously toward County Road 131. Fear took the place of curiosity, and—since her mother wasn't answering the phone—she called Theo.

For backup.

Not because she needed him, but because her mom had been right.

Theo was a good choice.

He'd agreed to meet her there—beat her there, even.

WHEN GRETCHEN PULLED up to the house, she saw that Dakota had been right to text her.

Something was off.

Her mom, Rhett Houston, Dakota, Ky, and Theo were standing in a loose ring near the porch.

Mr. Rhett's truck was parked out by the main road, but she carefully drove by it, eyeing the whole scene with suspicion until a dog meandered out into the middle of the drive. A big, black dog with a gray muzzle and ears.

Bewildered, Gretchen put the SUV in park and hopped out.

"Gretchen!" Theo called, anxiously.

He jogged up to her and wrapped her in a hug. And she hugged him back, pressing her cheek into the cove of his neck.

In just two short days, they'd figured things out. Romance... love—whatever it was, they were together.

A couple.

"Are you okay?" he whispered into her ear.

She shook her head and leaned back, "What is going *on*?"

Her eyes flashed up to her family and Rhett Houston, who were watching and waiting for them to rejoin.

Theo grabbed her hand and tugged her gently toward the group.

"What happened?" she asked again, to anyone who'd answer.

Her mother's lips pulled back in a grimace and her eyebrows etched lines into her forehead. "Sweetheart, come here."

Gretchen did as she was told, falling into a warm hug with her mother. Ky, oddly, joined in too, wrapping his arm around his sister's lower back and squeezing.

It was Dakota who answered, though. "Dad was here," he said, with the urgency that she had felt in his text message.

"What do you mean?" Gretchen replied.

Her mother cleared her throat and looked around at the faces waiting patiently for the full story. "Yes, Travis came here. He was under the influence and wanted to...well, he wanted to come back to us," she said at length.

Gretchen frowned. "*Come back*? We don't want him back, though." She eyed the boys with accusation, in spite of herself.

To her surprise, Ky nodded enthusiastically. Dakota blew air out of his mouth and scuffed the dirt with the toe of his tennis shoe.

Mr. Rhett shoved his hands into his pockets and sort of turned away from the group.

"No, we don't. You're right. But it's a good first step, don't you think?" her mom asked seriously.

Gretchen shook her head. "A good first step toward *what*?"

"Toward closure, for starters. And, maybe, a new normal?"

Gretchen blinked back tears she didn't know she had stored. In two short days, the tide had turned for her.

She was now certain she felt nothing for her father. Apathy. Indifference. That was all that was left. She had her full two weeks to process everything, and it had resulted squarely in the truth that she didn't care about him.

Period. Bottom line.

A tear worked its way loose and trickled down her cheek, smearing rivulets through her blush. She pressed the back of her hand to dry her skin and push the powder into place.

"What are you talking about?" she asked her mom, sniffles following the last syllable. Her head began to hurt. She thought about her practicum—the thing she had focused all of her dread onto. Because everything else *had* been resolved. At least, for a day. She was with Theo. Her father had left. They had a home. Rhett Houston was back in the city. Gretchen raised her voice. "*What* is going *on?*"

Her mother shushed her. "Gretchen, listen. He's gone. Your father is gone. We are still getting a divorce—hopefully soon. One day, maybe you all will want to visit him. But for now, nothing has changed. Except that he was here. For a short time, he was here. I gave him a piece of my mind, and he left, and that's it. Nothing more to be said of the matter." Her voice was even and smooth, as though she'd just emerged from a hot tub with a glass of wine cradled in her hand.

As though, for the first time in Gretchen's entire life, her mother was... at peace.

Tentative joy took anxiety's place in Gretchen's chest, and she allowed herself to smile at her mom.

The energy of their whole group shifted, and her mom began to change the tone, suggesting they order pizza and soda and have a little celebration.

Mr. Rhett excused himself, but Gretchen caught him lock eyes with her mom first.

For the first time in a while, Gretchen studied Maggie, *hard*. Her reddish hair had lost a little color. Wiry gray tendrils jutted out at her hairline, adding a witchy effect. Her face, bare and clean, seemed devoid of the age spots Gretchen had noticed just days prior. Freckles played out across her forehead and nose, even beneath her neatly waxed eyebrows.

Gretchen, throughout her life, had considered her mother the pinnacle of beauty and womanhood. A hairdresser who looked stylish in a pair of sweats and a lumpy t-shirt. She was a...*cool* mom, which Gretchen had sort of hated to admit.

But the past two weeks had shown a different side of her. The grit that Gretchen didn't know was there. The passion. The complexity. Complexity of being a modern woman in a small, rural town. Maggie had done it all.

And, Gretchen now saw, she had done it right.

Theo came up behind her as the others began planning a makeshift party. Gretchen turned to him.

"Hey," she whispered, letting him take her hand and pull her off.

They strode back toward the barn.

He gave her hand a squeeze and led her out of sight of the others. "Listen, Gretchen," he started, his eyes darting nervously.

"Yeah?" she asked.

"I did some research," he began.

Gretchen eyed him, nervous. "Research about what?"

Theo glanced around, avoiding her gaze. "About sewing stuff," he admitted at last.

Gretchen smiled.

He went on, "And I found out that they give night classes at the library. It's a women's group from Little Flock Catholic. They do night classes on Tuesday and Thursday. Six o'clock. Every week. I, uh, I signed you up."

Her smile fell away and she shook her head. "Theo, I still have practicum next week, and if I don't pass I might have to make up the hours—I can't do the sewing thing, and anyway..."

Theo held up a hand. "You need to quit beauty school, Gretchen." His face was solemn.

She said, "No, I can't. My mom wants me to do hair with her. It's supposed to be..."

"Our thing?"

It was her mother's voice behind them.

Gretchen nodded slowly. "Yeah. *Our thing*," she whispered, tears filling her eyes and blurring her vision.

"I wondered where you all went. I wasn't trying to spy or anything." She held her hands up helplessly then dropped them to her thighs.

A bitter wind pushed Gretchen closer to her mother, and she glanced back at Theo, who just nodded.

"I talked to Theo," Maggie said.

Gretchen stayed quiet.

"Or, I guess you could say *he*," she nodded back to Gretchen's new boyfriend, "talked to *me*."

Theo coughed in the background before shuffling awkwardly back toward the farmhouse.

Maggie reached out and tucked a strand of Gretchen's blonde hair behind her ear. It tickled, and a single tear spilled over her eyelid and down her cheek. She swallowed.

"I'm really sorry, Gretch."

Gretchen frowned. "Sorry for what?"

"Well, everything, for starters. But specifically pushing you into a career that wasn't yours."

They were silent for a minute, Gretchen glancing around, uncomfortable about the truth. Maggie crossing her arms over her chest and rocking back and forth against the cold. Uncertain what to say, the former finally replied, "It's fine, Mom."

"No, it's not. I just—I don't want to give you an excuse here, but I didn't know what else was out there, and I didn't want you to leave our house thinking you had to rely on a boyfriend. I wanted you to turn nineteen and have something in place. I think," Maggie paused, searching for words. "I think I didn't have a strong role model. Marguerite was a good woman, and she took good care of us. But she was in survival mode, and I think she had been since I was born. Dirk and I were sort of just shoved at her. She didn't have a choice. And then, she raised us like that. Like she didn't have a choice. Which was hard. I wanted you—and I wanted your brothers and sister *so* much, but I was also *very* scared."

Gretchen frowned. "Of Dad?"

"No, no. I was never afraid of Travis. I mean, he was controlling. That's for sure. But I knew he wasn't good enough for me or for you all." Her mom sniffed. "And I was afraid I'd been a bad role model to you in a different way than Marguerite had been to me."

"Mom, you *are* a great role model."

Maggie shook her head. "I'm going to do better. And speaking of which, hair doesn't have to be 'our thing.' Maybe *this*," her mom gestured to the property, "could be *our* thing," she whispered, pulling Gretchen into a deep hug and kissing her head. "I love you, Gretchen."

Gretchen smiled, nodded, and whispered back, "I love you, too, Mom."

They parted and walked back toward the farmhouse, their arms wrapped around each other's waists.

"Oh, by the way," her mother said, before they walked up the porch to join the others inside.

"Yeah?"

"I found something today. Something I think you'll like."

Gretchen eyed her mother suspiciously and they walked in through the door to the loud chatter of the boys arguing over what flavor of pizza to order.

Maggie turned Gretchen up the staircase and into the second bedroom, freshly scrubbed and awaiting a new coat of paint. It smelled like wood varnish and Windex.

There, in the far corner, stood a beautiful, perfect, Singer sewing machine. Table, pedal, and all.

Gretchen gasped.

"And one more thing, Gretch," her mom said as Gretchen crossed the floor feverishly. "I think Theo's right. Maybe it's time to quit beauty school, after all."

Chapter 32 — Rhett

"Two cheese, two pepperonis, and two liters of root beer," Rhett confirmed with the boys as he withdrew his phone from his pocket to call the pizza parlor.

Ky smiled gratefully at Rhett, and he returned the expression and offered a high five. "You all handled that situation really well, you know."

Dakota shrugged his shoulders. "We're used to it."

Rhett cocked his head. "Used to what?"

"Crazy stuff," Ky replied on his brother's behalf, lifting a conspiratorial eyebrow to Rhett.

He chuckled and exchanged a look with Theo, who sat patiently at the table. "Is that so?"

"Oh yeah," Dakota went on. "Every single person in the family is a little crazy. Just to warn you," he added with emphasis.

"What do you mean 'warn' me?"

Ky sighed dramatically. "If you're going to hang around here, then you'd better know about it. Okay?"

Warmth flooded Rhett's chest, and he didn't realize how badly he wanted validation from a set of goof-off pre-teen boys. "Well," he began as he heard Maggie and Gretchen descend down the stairs in time for someone to knock at the front door.

"I can handle that. But I won't be around here much, so you don't have to worry about me, okay?"

The two boys scrunched their faces at him. "Why not?"

"Yeah, Mr. Rhett, *why not?*" It was Maggie's voice, behind him.

Rhett spun around to see her grinning at him, her arms crossed as she winked at her sons. Beyond Maggie, Gretchen opened the door to a giggly Briar with Becky in tow.

He couldn't believe he'd let so many years go by without staying part of his friends' lives.

Then, he glanced back to Maggie. Her naked beauty. Her strength. Her wit... her *everything*. And he realized why.

It was too painful.

"I'm in the middle of a house search, and Old Gray is really hoping I can get him a yard with grass."

"We have grass!" Briar piped up, climbing into her mom's arms excitedly. "We have grass out there, Mr. Rhett!" she pointed out the four-pane window of the kitchen door toward the little chicken coop with the single, wild-eyed chicken.

Beneath the thin layer of thawing frost, she was right, there was grass. Soggy, pale grass. The farm wasn't entirely dried out. It had life left. Waiting for them.

All those years, Maggie's family farmhouse had been sitting out there in secret, waiting for the day a lively family would tumble in and bring it back to life.

Becky, awkwardly, announced she had somewhere to be. Maggie hugged her and saw her to the door.

The kids dispersed about the house, finding new places to explore and new things to do.

Theo and Gretchen decided to go check on the chicken.

Maggie returned slowly to Rhett. Her breath slow. Her eyes tired. Her whole being... *happy*?

"Hey," he said to her, his voice low.

"Hey," she answered.

"Listen, Maggie, I better go. You've got your hands full here, and I need to get back to the city. Feed my dog." He rubbed a hand over the lower half of his face and glanced away.

She nodded. "You're right."

Rhett locked eyes to see her staring hard at him. He swallowed.

Maggie looked away. "I do have my hands full."

"I'm just a phone call away. If you need anything, give me a buzz. I'll be here."

Her lips turned down. "Oh, right," she answered, pressing her hands into her pockets.

Rhett licked his lips. "Glad everything's working out for you, Maggie."

"Yeah," she said. "We'll see, I guess."

And with that, he bent down and gave her half a hug. Not the full-frontal hug with a side of kiss that he desperately *needed* to give her. Instead, a side brush that would ensure he didn't lose his mind. That would ensure he could let go.

He strode to the door, leaving her in the kitchen.

Old Gray met him at the base of the porch, thumping his tail through the air with old-dog anticipation. But he didn't follow Rhett back to the truck. Not right away. He sort of ambled off right, panting his way toward the back of the farm.

Rhett whistled for him, walking slowly in the direction of his truck out by the main road.

Old Gray stood at the corner where the house met the side of the property. It gave Rhett a wide view of all that Maggie now had. Her land. Her home. Her *family*.

And he knew that it was everything he wanted.

And everything he couldn't have.

"Gray, let's go," he called, slapping his thighs at the dog, who promptly fell into a lazy sit.

Rhett shook his head, but his phone buzzed to life in his pocket, putting off the confrontation momentarily.

He pulled the thin device out, and—without looking at the screen—answered.

"I need something."

A smile tugged at the corners of his lips.

It was her.

He played along. "Oh?"

The front door opened in front of him, and Maggie stepped out, her phone to her ear. "Heat," she answered him.

Rhett felt blood pulse through his body. "*Heat?*" he replied, his voice cracking on the line as he glanced around, keeping an eye out for the kids. His gaze returned to Maggie, whose fingers, he noticed for the first time since he'd reunited with her weeks earlier, were all bare.

She nodded and purred back into the line. "Hot water, I mean."

His body relaxed and he smiled broadly up at her, dropping the phone to his side. "What do you mean, hot water?"

"We don't have any. And," she answered, her eyes dancing circles as he walked back to the porch, and stood at the bottom, staring up at her. "Can you help me install a water heater?"

"Sure," he answered. "Tell me a day and time. I'll be here."

"Today. Now," she answered, stepping down toward him.

He sucked in a deep breath. "All right. Well, we can hit the hardware store in town, see what they have. We could always start tomorrow. I could check out one of the wholesale warehouses in Louisville, if you—"

She held up a hand. "Rhett, I have an idea."

"Oh?"

"Why don't you stay here?" Maggie waved a hand out.

Rhett fell back a step. "Aw, no. I can't do that, Maggie. You've got a full house. And I have my studio. And a new place popped up on the market just north of the city. I'm heading over to check it out in the morning..."

But she wasn't going to take no for answer. "Rhett, stay here. You can sleep in the parlor once we move the mattresses upstairs. The kids won't care. It'll be fun, and I could really use your help for a few days. I'd hate for you to drive back and forth."

"Maggie, I can't. You're still—" He caught himself. That wasn't the real issue. The real issue was something else. "I have a place in Louisville. And my rentals are there. Besides, Maggie, I'm no live-in handyman. You know?"

She nodded slowly. "I see."

"No, no. It's not what you think. I would *love* to live with you." His chest constricted and his pace quickened. The truth was pushing through, and all Rhett wanted was for them to confront it. But *right then*? *Right there*?

"But what?" she answered, her palms open.

He racked his brain for a good answer, fully aware that he could never tell her the real reasons. Because he loved her. Because she was still married. Because he was a provider and could never live in her barn like some sort of hired man.

"Oh," she said at last. "I get it." The light went out of her eyes, and she took a step back. "You don't... you don't want to..."

He frowned. "Wait, Maggie, what? No, it's not—"

"You don't want to complicate things. I'm still married. It's weird. I... get it. I can find someone else."

It was the impetus he needed. Maggie couldn't afford to find someone else. She didn't need one more thing on her plate.

And just like that, when it occurred to Rhett that his living at the farm wasn't about who he was as a man but instead about who he was as a person, he knew what he had to do.

"You know what?" he replied before she made it to the first step, ready to wave goodbye forever. "I'm being ridiculous. Of course I can stay here."

Her face lit up and she rushed into his arms, knocking him backwards. It was a full-on hug. The one he worried he couldn't handle.

"But on one condition," he said as she pushed back, glowing with excitement.

"Whatever it is, sure," she answered, clapping giddily.

Rhett smiled and jutted his chin out past the house toward the barn. "I'll stay in there."

Chapter 33 — Maggie

They agreed he would start in two weeks.

In the meantime, more trips to Becky's for hot showers. And each of those trips was more than just a quick pop in and out. It would include an oversized down-home meal—the boys certainly didn't complain about that—in addition to a new round of convincing Memaw that Becky's "impulse chicken" (whom the kids had taken to calling Greg) in fact *added* to their family. There was no more need for Memaw to nag and ridicule Becky about it. Maggie declared over and again she was happy to keep the chicken.

She had a farm after all.

And, in fact, she considered getting a few more.

March was near at hand, and Maggie figured that since she'd gotten back on track with her clients—it turned out the kitchen was just as good a place to do hair as anywhere else in Hickory Grove, Indiana. She now had enough extra money to start settling in for the long haul.

With no mortgage and a forest's worth of trees to harvest for the fireplace, bills were lower in the farmhouse than they'd ever been in a dual-income house on Pine Tree Lane. And, what was more, if Maggie could put up a little money to secure real, working livestock, then she could start supplying their own groceries right there at the farm.

That wasn't to speak of a garden or any crops—though the latter was not likely to happen.

Still, Maggie turned out to be something of a green thumb. Especially with the help of her growing children who seemed acutely interested in country life, much to Maggie's happy surprise.

Using the outhouse was the biggest adjustment, but Maggie had to admit it was tenable. At least for a little while longer—until Rhett was to show up with his truck bed full of tools.

Maggie spent her days painting as the kids came and went from school. Briar, who had since convinced her mother to get a kitten, mostly occupied herself in the parlor, playing house with the little cat while Maggie passed from room to room, touching up spots she had missed.

Thoughts of Rhett filled Maggie's head, but she pushed them away as hard as she could. Though she no longer wore her wedding band, and though Travis had signed his paperwork, she was still married for the time being. They still had to appear for court and take parenting classes. It would be a few months until the deal was done.

But even more than an incomplete divorce, Maggie had her children to think of. Two daughters and two sons. And she did not want to set the example that a woman was only happy when she was with a man.

Sure, partners could enhance one's life, Maggie reiterated over breakfast on the one morning Dakota had, much to her surprise, brought it up. However, the Engel family needed time to take care of each other first. They needed time to unpack. Time to settle.

The kids had all scoffed at that. Ky even said, *"We've already done all that!"*

But her answer came quickly: Rhett would be living there soon enough. And once he moved in, nothing would change.

Other than their plumbing situation.

Of course, none of those rationalizations changed what Maggie felt deep down. What her heart told her.

But God had opened a window for the now single mom. And she was committed to doing things right.

And doing things right took time.

Especially, when one was waiting for a divorce.

But then, late in the afternoon of Friday, a phone call came in.

IT WAS BECKY, WHO DECLARED she was on the speaker phone with Zack Durbin, Esquire.

And they had news.

"You were never married."

Maggie fell into the armchair in the parlor, only half listening as she bit down into a crisp, red apple.

Becky started to repeat herself until Zack took the phone and did it for her. "Maggie, this is Zack. Your marriage license was never filed in the state of Indiana. Do you know anything about that?"

Maggie nearly choked. "What?"

"Just what I said. There is no record of your having married Travis Wayne Engel in the state of Indiana. Did you get married across state lines? In Louisville, maybe?"

"We got married at Little Flock right here in town. It was a private ceremony. Marguerite kept it that way since I was pregnant." Her voice trembled through the recollection. "We signed the paper. I remember it. We even have a certificate from the church," she said, standing and darting to the staircase to head upstairs and grab the offending document.

"Did you send it to the county to be recorded?" Zack asked urgently.

Maggie stalled at the top of the staircase. "I don't know. I don't remember. I never went to the courthouse or anything, if that's what you mean."

"Did Travis?"

"Did he what?" Maggie asked, her mind shuffling through history and catching up to the present, desperate to understand.

"Did Travis have your marriage recorded? Did Marguerite send it?"

She shook her head. "I don't know. I—I don't know."

"You got married here, at Little Flock Catholic? In *Hickory Grove*?" Zack emphasized the final words of his question.

Nodding her head vehemently, she answered, "Yes, I'm positive. A private ceremony. Father Dan. Little Flock. Yes."

"Maggie, do you know what this means?" Zack asked, his voice quiet and patient.

Overcome with confusion and elation, she replied that no, admittedly, she did not.

"I already left a voicemail with Travis's attorney to confirm, but if you two didn't have the marriage recorded, then it's akin to fraud."

"*Fraud?*" Maggie gasped. The implications swirled around her. Was she a criminal? Was Travis?

"It's okay; it's okay. This has happened before. You won't get in trouble, but it makes anything in your life tied to your marriage null and void. It grants you, effectively, an annulment."

She swallowed and her eyes glassed over with tears. "I'm not married to Travis?"

Becky came back on the line through the speaker, her voice a whisper. "You never were, sweetheart."

RHETT ARRIVED JUST when he said he would. His truck bed boasted only a few large boxes. On the trailer hitched behind him was everything else.

And truly, everything. Lawn mower, weed eater, metal tool chest tied into submission onto the floor of the trailer.

And, sitting squarely in the middle of it all, two massive boxes.

One water heater.

And one toilet.

He was a hero.

Maggie greeted Rhett with some distance, offering a broad smile and a hello, and then calling forth Old Gray, who she proceeded to give a good belly rub.

Rhett hollered a hello to the kids, who were prancing about, delighted at the unseasonably warm winter day.

The children waved happily back and carried on.

Gretchen was at the back of the property with Theo, stacking firewood.

Briar's kitten perched on the top of the porch, eyeing Old Gray with circumspection.

"Think they'll get along?" Maggie teased Rhett, gesturing to the two pets.

He grinned. "Opposites sometimes attract. They'll figure it out."

Maggie nodded. "I have good news and bad news," she announced, anxious to spill everything to him, now that she had him there in person.

"Oh?" he replied.

"Which do you want first?"

Rhett inhaled then let out his breath as though the matter were a serious one. "I abide by the low expectations rule, usually."

"What's that?" she answered, nearing him as he worked to free his tool chest from its pinned position on the bed of the trailer.

"Always start with the bad news. Then, everything that follows is good."

"Oh, so you're that type, huh?" She held out her hand for the ropes he'd finished loosening. He passed them over, and she began to wrap them in wide loops from her shoulder to elbow. It was one of those rare talents Maggie possessed—rope-looping—back when she had the energy to tackle yard work at Pine Tree Lane.

That same energy had returned to her recently, and she'd welcomed it.

Rhett took the bait. "What type?"

"The patient type. You can hold out. You aren't afraid you might die and miss the good stuff."

He chuckled. "Well, when you put it that way..."

They locked eyes for a moment, and then the shrill of children's laughter broke in.

Maggie went on. "Okay, the bad news. I still haven't gotten the lock to bust open on the barn. I have no idea what is in there, and I have done exactly nothing in the way of setting up for you." She felt her cheeks grow warm.

It was an honest admission, but it wasn't her style. She liked to have things ready for guests. Her work station was always primed for clients. But she didn't have the tools or time to see about cracking into the barn.

It had fallen off her to-do list.

Rhett didn't react much, though. "No big deal. I can get it open. It'll be a fun adventure," he added with a wink.

"You can sleep in the parlor until we have the barn set up," she added, nervous.

He simply nodded, his eyes fixed on the task of righting the chest of drawers and centering it on his dolly.

"What's the good news?" he asked at length, now easing the teetering chest down the ramp.

Maggie rushed in to steady the left side and helped him drop the unit to the ground.

Again, their gazes caught, and she answered him. "It's Travis. The divorce. It, well..." Maggie had practiced how she was going to deliver the news all night and all morning, but there she was, fudging it all up.

"What is it?" Rhett pressed, his face falling a little.

She shook her head. "Um, what I mean is... well, we aren't married. We never were. He didn't file the license. Everything was a sham, inadvertently."

Rhett's eyes widened and his mouth fell open a little. He asked for more information, and she unloaded it, explaining that she'd used the church certificate for her name change with various entities, such as beauty school. But, she never *did* get around to updating her name on her driver's license or social security card due to pure laziness.

And that was it. Maggie's life was so small and so centered around those who already *knew* her that she needed no further proof that she belonged to Travis.

Or, at least, that was the case for so many years.

But it worked out. And when she went to claim the farmhouse, her name wasn't an issue, because Marguerite hadn't left the property to Dirk Devereux and Margaret Engel.

She'd left it to *Margaret Devereux.*

Even though Maggie had been "married" to Travis for years by the time the old woman had written it.

"Do you think...?" Rhett began.

Maggie lifted her shoulders. "Maybe. I guess Travis told his attorney that, back then, that my aunt said she'd deliver the license to the courthouse for us. But she never did."

RHETT'S RELIEF AT HER news was palpable, as though he had an answer to a question he'd been waiting years to ask. But never did.

Turned out, he didn't need to ask. He just needed that patience he so clearly possessed.

Now, as they finished unloading his truck, they turned their attention to the new project at hand: the barn.

"Let's see what we've got," Rhett muttered, pulling a conveniently packed bolt cutter from beneath the back seat of the cab of his truck.

Maggie followed him silently, breathing in the almost-spring air and exhaling it deeply.

Things were good. The kids were happy. Gretchen had quit night classes and started working on her "craft," as she cleverly referred to it. Mostly, the poor thing hadn't gotten far. The old Singer was missing parts, and Maggie was useless in troubleshooting.

Fern Gale had come over to help, suggesting they order a new machine and start over again. But Gretchen refused, asserting that she was meant to use the Devereux heirloom.

She'd searched high and low in the few cupboards and cabinets of the old farmhouse, coming up empty each day. She'd begun researching which parts to order, but she was hesitant to spend her hard-earned money just yet.

Gretchen's budding hobby aside, the boys were in better spirits than they'd ever been. The fresh air clearly did them something good, but it was more than that. Like a burden had been lifted. The burden of an unhealthy marriage (or, relationship, as the case may have been) between their parents, perhaps.

Surprising to Maggie, was how excited they were to welcome Rhett to the property. They'd cleaned their room from top to bottom and begged their mom to get a new dog bed for Old Gray. She'd declined, to their crushing disappointment, but now she was having second thoughts. Maybe they would need a dog bed since Rhett and Old Gray might be in the farmhouse with them.

Presently, the chickens (yes, they'd "adopted" more) squabbled in the distance, and Maggie noticed the boys off in the distance, trying to catch Rhett's attention as they whipped a baseball back and forth, a rhythmic thud echoing over to the barn as the ball hit each leather mitt in succession.

Briar whined briefly, then gave up and went off to search for Lady Kitten, her new best friend.

Rhett saw the boys and called out to them. "Nice form, guys!"

Maggie could have sworn Ky's face reddened with pride.

Dakota, more assured, answered, "Come play in a while, Mr. Rhett!"

The question hit Maggie in the heart, and it occurred to her that she never once saw Travis play with either boy. And, of course, never his daughters.

"I sure will!" Rhett hollered back. "Give me half an hour, all right?"

Dakota and Ky both threw a thumbs up, and Maggie allowed herself solace. Even if Rhett was only there for a spell—even if he was only ever a live-in handyman—at least the boys would have a man there. A good man. A role model.

Rhett popped the padlock with relative ease and looked back to Maggie. "She's ready," he declared, a playful grin dancing on his lips.

Her pulse quickened, and Rhett stood back to let her open the barn door slowly.

Maggie stopped and looked back over her shoulder to the house. "Hang on," she told Rhett. "Gretchen needs to see this."

She held her hands to her mouth and hollered as loudly as she could, her voice carrying to the farmhouse.

Gretchen's face appeared in the kitchen door window. Maggie gestured for her to join them, and Gretchen did, exiting the door and letting the screen slap shut before striding with purpose toward the barn.

When she arrived, Maggie gestured toward the rusty lock, now lying inert on the ground.

"You ready?" she asked her daughter.

Gretchen nodded, smiling from Rhett to Maggie.

Again, Maggie hooked her fingers in the handle and tugged. The heavy wood scraped along the ground. Rhett came up behind her and pulled the door from above her head.

Though darker inside the barn, two high, round windows allowed modest light to fill the wide, high cavern.

Maggie and Gretchen gasped.

Neatly stacked milk crates intermixed with boxes on top of wooden pallets that had long succumbed to dry rot.

A musty stench tickled Maggie's nose, and she sneezed.

Old haystacks towered to the right, across from the pallets that had nearly sunk into the dirt floor beneath their boxes.

Some pieces of furniture sat at odd angles in the loft above.

What once had been a stable became visible in the far back of the space as their eyes grew accustomed to the shadows.

"Look," Gretchen whispered as she neared the boxes.

Maggie joined her. On every single cardboard box, the material of which had begun to disintegrate in the damp barn, was printed in thick, clear letters:

Camille Devereux.

Gretchen pressed her fingers to the name and looked back at her mother, who nodded.

Boxes and crates.

Memories.

Hope.

Maybe even answers.

But one single feeling filled Maggie's chest in that moment.

Peace.

And two words that in her life she'd so rarely used together, finally fell from Maggie's lips. "*My mom.*"

Chapter 34 — Maggie

Three Months Later.

It had taken weeks, but with the help of Rhett, Gretchen, and even Theo, they had cleared out the lower part of the barn and had even begun on the loft.

A cellar beneath the house made for proper storage, and that was where Maggie carefully transferred and laid to rest many of her mother's possessions, including clothing and garments that weren't too terribly moth-eaten, a few books, and other personal effects.

Devereux family documents, neatly filed into plastic bins, now rested on sturdy shelves down there, too, courtesy of Rhett and Theo, the latter of whom had taken up something of a casual weekend apprenticeship in the craft of all things home improvements.

He'd confessed to everyone that his dad was more of an indoor guy, and he was excited to learn about real work.

Rhett had loved that.

So did Gretchen.

And Maggie loved that Theo and Gretchen had become serious. It wouldn't have occurred to her that she'd like to see her daughter settle down so early in life, but she was now able to see that the sins of the mother weren't always passed on.

With any luck, in fact, Maggie had turned the tide for the family. After taking pains to keep Rhett at arm's length, things had slowly grown comfortable. Delicately comfortable.

He moved from the parlor to the barn once they had added flooring and basic amenities, and it opened a space the family needed to fully settle in.

But, it also opened an absence, and no sooner than he had a sofa and a television set in the makeshift workshop did they invite him right back for supper every evening, movie nights every Tuesday and Friday.

And, of course, there was no plumbing in the barn, yet. So, Rhett still had a place in the shower rotation, further entrenching him into the oversized family routine.

Still, while the family had become used to him, Rhett never seemed as perfectly at home as Maggie would have liked.

And she would have liked that. Very much.

Especially when Gretchen, one night, professed to love that they had Rhett around.

"He makes me feel safe," she whispered to her mother when the two were lounging in Maggie's bed chatting airily into the late hours.

"Me, too," Maggie replied.

Gretchen sat up. "Mom?"

"Yeah, Gretch?"

"Are you ever going to start dating him?"

Maggie squeezed her eyes shut, her cheeks reddening at her daughter's suggestion. "Oh, Gretchen. I don't know. He's a good man, but he's just here to help."

"We have a toilet, now," Gretchen pointed out before adding, "and a water heater."

"So?"

"So what else does he need to help with?"

"The barn, remember?" Maggie answered plainly.

The plan was to add plumbing and enclose the loft as a sort of second floor in the barn. It could be Gretchen's apartment and sewing house. She'd live there as long as she needed. It would be her own little place, complete with a working sewing table and craft space, solid oak bookshelves stuffed to the brim with Gretchen's many titles, and comfortable enough to host guests, such as Theo... if the time ever came.

Gretchen smiled. "Yeah, but that's a big project. Expensive, too. And we haven't even finished sorting through the boxes."

It was true.

Maggie let out a long sigh. She wanted so badly to read every last paper, scour every last note in the few boxes that remained in the loft of the barn. They weren't family documents.

They were Camille Devereux's private collection. At least, that's what Maggie had assumed when they stumbled upon them and tested their weight. Not full-but-light with garments. Not over-heavy and loaded down with the books.

They were the weight of history.

The history of Camille's short life.

Maggie could tell.

But she couldn't read them and find out.

Because if Maggie didn't open the boxes, then she always had something to look forward to.

She always had more to learn.

More to know about where she came from.

"Why don't you at least open them?" Gretchen asked, reaching across the comforter toward the bowl of popcorn resting in Maggie's lap.

"I will. I just... I want *time*. You know?"

"Time for what? Aren't you curious? Maybe there are, like, pictures in there."

"Maybe," Maggie replied. "But I want to really have time to bring them in here, sit down, and spread everything out."

"You have time, Mom," Gretchen pushed. "Just do it, already."

Maggie considered this. Time, she had. Maybe that wasn't it. Maybe something else was keeping her from the task.

Like fear.

"MORNIN'."

Rhett stood just beyond the threshold of her front door. It was eight o'clock on an otherwise average Monday in late May.

A sunny, warm day.

The type of day that made Maggie want to unearth her bathing suit, grab a towel, and sprawl out on the grass like a sun-thirsty teenager hoping for the perfect tan.

But Maggie was not a teenager any more.

No matter how much Rhett, standing there in his worn Levi's and snug-fitting white t-shirt, made her feel like one.

"You really don't have to knock anymore, you know," she said, smiling from ear to ear.

He shrugged, grinning back. "Sorry, but I can't *not* knock."

Maggie stepped aside. "Come on in. Breakfast is nearly ready," she directed.

Rhett's smile faded. "Actually," he replied, "I can't join you today."

She frowned. "Oh?" Her plans for the morning flashed through her mind. He was going to start the bathroom that week. Gretchen had picked out a bathtub, even. But Maggie wasn't in the position to remind him about any of that.

"I, uh..." he licked his lips, and his eyes darted about the front porch, landing on Old Gray, snoring in the far corner. "I was going to go take a look at a place out in Corydon today."

Her mouth fell open, and she quickly shut it.

Maggie knew this was coming. Rhett had said over and again that he was going to start house hunting soon.

She didn't know he already *was*.

"Oh," she replied, swallowing.

He took a deep breath. "Maggie, listen," he began, avoiding her stare. "I don't want to impose on your family any longer."

"Impose? You're not imposing on us, Rhett. Don't be ridiculous. You... I mean, you're *part* of our family now." She waved her hand back behind her as Dakota and Ky conveniently descended the staircase.

"Look," he said, pinning her with a steely gaze. "I'll be back this afternoon. We can talk more then." Rhett added a broad smile and waved at the boys, who, unaware of a mounting and unpredicted tension, trudged into the kitchen for breakfast.

Maggie nodded at Rhett before he turned to go.

Once the boys had passed and Rhett was on the bottom step, she moved through the door and stopped him. "Rhett," she said, her voice low and firm.

He turned, his expression weary. "Maggie, I can't do this anymore." He held his palms up at his sides. "I love it here. I love being near you. All of you. But I need my own life, too. I'll finish the barn. You don't have to worry about that—"

"I don't give a crud about the *barn*," she answered, hopping down the steps and joining him on the grass. "I just—" But it was useless. What could Maggie possibly say?

Over weeks—*months*—of silent flirtations during movie nights, painfully teasing eye contact across the kitchen table, and little touches here and there as they hammered and drilled and painted and scrubbed... nothing emerged.

Maggie never once showed up at the barn after dinner. She'd never once sent him a private text message about something other than what to buy at the hardware store. She'd never once taken an opportunity to tell him that, yes, there was more to it. More to all of it.

She never once told Rhett that their situation was *not* a temporary arrangement or that she wanted it to be permanent.

As far as Rhett knew, he was a live-in handyman.

But that wasn't who Rhett was. And Maggie knew it.

Chapter 35 — Rhett

"I don't want to pressure you into anything, Maggie. But I can't do this anymore." Rhett kept his voice low and soft.

He looked past her for a moment, then took a step closer, his body just inches from hers. He could smell her shampoo from that spot. He could breathe her in, and he wanted to. So badly.

Which was why he had to go.

"Can't do what?" she asked.

Finally. It was out there. An opportunity for the truth.

"Maggie, I can't be near you if I can't be *with* you." He blew out a breath and squeezed both eyes shut before cracking one open like a kid, nervous to admit it was *his* baseball that broke the kitchen window.

Her face fell for a moment. And it was the answer he hated to have but knew he needed.

It was a "no."

Plain and simple.

"I brought down a couple of the boxes from the loft. Figured you could go through them. Or not. But if we can get them down, things will go faster. Sound good?"

He tried to smile, but it wouldn't come, and Rhett realized that weeks of pretending that he could just be there and help had taken their toll.

Sure, it began that way. A win-win. He had a place to stay while he found a home to buy. Maggie had his help.

But the feelings grew strong and deep.

What made it all worse was that he *knew* Maggie felt the same.

But she refused to accept it. Or face it. Or deal with it.

Either that, or she was afraid. And Rhett knew nothing he did could ease those fears. Because he'd spent all those weeks and months showing her that she had nothing to fear.

And yet she was still afraid.

"Rhett, don't go," Maggie whispered, reaching her hand out and resting it on his forearms.

He licked his lips and closed his eyes. After a deep breath, he tried again. "I'm not going anywhere. If this place works out, it'll be a month or two before I close. We'll finish your project and everything will be fine. Right?"

She lifted her shoulders and shook her head, a million questions in her eyes. But none of them came out. Instead just, "Yeah. Thanks."

Again, he pointed toward the boxes he'd pulled down. "If you all get the rest out today, we'll have a chance to get rolling with the loft."

Rhett scanned the property, shoved his hands into his pockets, and slowly walked to his truck.

Chapter 36 — Maggie

I t was a slap in the face.

Rhett, effectively, was moving on.

Despite all their happiness, he could not stay. Not without more.

And Maggie wanted all the things he did. Truly. But something still tugged on her heart. On her conscience.

It wasn't the kids.

They loved Rhett.

It wasn't Travis.

The custody arrangement was in place and fine.

It was something in Maggie. Deep inside her.

After a brief breakfast, she saw the kids off to school and bid Gretchen a good day at work then returned to the farm alone.

And then Maggie went to the barn. Where those boxes sat. The ones with *Camille Devereux* scrawled neatly across the sides.

The ones with the weight of history.

The ones Maggie was scared to death to open.

The ones she had to open now. Even if they revealed nothing. Even if they revealed a horrible truth.

Maggie had to dig into her history and clear the cobwebs.

Or else she wouldn't have a future.

Swallowing and opening the refinished barn door, Maggie marveled at all they'd accomplished together.

A waxed wood floor sprawled beyond a simple apron entrance. Rhett's sleeper sofa squarely against the left wall, facing an organized entertainment center, where his television sat next to a coffee pot and pair of mugs. A few books lined the shelves beneath the television, and Rhett's wardrobe stood on the far side, at the other edge of a patterned, navy blue rug.

For a barn studio, he'd made a nice home.

Maggie eyed three boxes sitting next to the front door. Instead of carting them back to the house, she dragged each of them over to the sofa, sat, and pressed her hands to the top.

It had been folded and taped, but she found it easy to pop her car key into one edge of the seam and drag it through the length.

Inside were books and doodads. A wooden jewelry box was tucked tightly along the far side, but all that was in it were a few costume pieces that meant no more to Maggie than they clearly did to her surviving parents and sister.

Maggie moved on to the next box, lingering over exactly what Gretchen had predicted: photo albums. Cloudy, dust-clogged plastic sleeves, largely empty.

The few photos that existed within the top three albums sat proudly in the first few pages, as though Maggie's mother intended to fill each album eventually.

But she never had the chance.

The two bottom albums were entirely devoid of photographs but instead held a few old school report cards.

Maggie poured over every image, every letter grade.

Her mother was beautiful. Blonde, in fact, if the black-and-white polaroids weren't entirely invalid. She looked nothing like Maggie.

Nothing at all.

Maggie continued to scour the images, searching for another face. A second face. A new face.

But it wasn't there.

She moved on to the third box, punching the seal and dragging the key through the worn, gummy tape with ease.

The third box was light, and once she peered inside, she saw why.

Only three things sat within: another photo album, a plastic bag with a piece of jewelry inside, and a notebook.

Overwhelmed with what she might learn, Maggie felt blood rush to her ears, drowning out the squabbling chickens and bleating goats.

Drowning out Old Gray's barks and Lady the Kitten's mews.

Drowning out the hum of a truck, rumbling up the lane toward the farmhouse.

Maggie reached her hands into the box and first withdrew the plastic baggie.

Inside, a tinny set of dog tags hung lightly at the bottom of a tiny ball chain.

Army dog tags.

Belonging to a man by the name of Joseph Merkle.

At first, the name meant nothing to Maggie. He could be anyone.

And yet something told her that Joseph Merkle wasn't just anyone.

Next, she withdrew the photo album.

Similar to the others, this one had but few photos. Some of Maggie's mother when she was young. Looking sullen and moody.

One of Mimi and Papa, sitting upright at a table, unsmiling.

And one of Camille with a boy. And it wasn't black and white, either.

It was as colorful as the day was bright.

Which was nice, because the boy wasn't some blurry, flat figure with his arm draped casually over her mother's shoulder.

He was a real, strong-jawed, fire-headed, freckle-faced man, whose glowing smile told Maggie who those dog tags belonged to.

Who Joseph Merkle was.

Maggie set the photo neatly on her lap and rubbed her eyes. It made no sense.

If her mother was with this Joseph person, why was it some big secret? And what happened to him? How did Camille come to keep the dog tags? Why were they tucked away in this box—a box that had been locked up in the barn and left to rot?

What was the big deal? Maggie wondered to herself.

The pounding in her ears had ebbed, and she heard a car engine die off outside.

Her time was almost up.

She grabbed the notebook and flipped it open.

There, consuming a great majority of the unlined cream pages was the even, leaning script of Camille Devereux.

She'd used the notebook as a journal. A diary. Dating each entry and signing them, too.

Frantic to know everything she could before the uninvited guest barged in on her, Maggie shuffled through the pages, skimming and scanning and seeing that, sometimes, her mother signed her name as Camille Merkle.

It was confirmation, but Maggie still wanted more.

"What happened to Joseph?" She murmured into the notebook as the sound of movement neared the barn.

And then she saw it. Dated precisely two months before Maggie's birthday: a final entry.

Maggie's eyes absorbed the words with fervor.

January 4, 1975

A letter came today. It was addressed to Mother and Father, but the information was for me, of course. My suspicions are now confirmed. Joe's dead. He's not M.I.A. He's not a P.O.W. He's none of those hopeful initialisms they tell us about. He's just dead, and now I don't know what I'll do. How can I be a mother without Joe?

My due date is near. I have no hope of happiness. I have no one to raise my family with. All I have are my austere parents and cruel sister. The same people who are kicking me out of my own house! They say I did all of this on purpose.

Well, I loved him on purpose, didn't I?

So I suppose they are right.

Joe told me he would propose. He told me he'd come back, and we would get married and go start our own farm together, away from them. He told me we would have a happy family and make our own way in this world. He told me he would be okay.

But now neither of us are. None of us are.

At least, I'll have my baby.

A tear formed in the corner of Maggie's eye as she read and reread her mother's words. Marguerite had said they didn't know Camille was having twins, but it had never seemed as interesting a note as when Maggie read her own mother's words on the matter.

Despite having the truth at long last, despite knowing that her father died in war and her mother in childbirth, all she could dwell on were her mother's penultimate thoughts.

None of us are.

"Are you okay?"

It was Rhett.

Strong, kind, patient-but-not-patient-enough Rhett.

Maggie looked up, and the tear spilled down her cheek, drying along her neck. She smiled. "Yes. Actually. I am."

Her stomach churned at the sight of him. His forehead creased and his eyes were wide. "What is it?" he asked.

"I just... I found some of my mother's things," she began then blinked. "Weren't you driving to Corydon?"

He closed the barn door behind him and joined her on the sofa, sitting precariously on the edge, all his weight on the heels of his feet, his jeans stretched tightly across his thighs.

Maggie met his gaze.

"Maggie, I'm frozen. I hate what I told you. I hate where we are." He looked down at her notebook and then to the other things sitting neatly on the sofa between them. "What is this stuff?" he asked, distracted by his own concern.

She smiled and set the notebook down on her other side, picking up the dog tags and photo album together. "It's my dad," she answered, lifting her shoulders and looking into Rhett's eyes, which had grown misty. "Are *you* okay?" she asked, dipping her chin and peering at him from beneath her eyelashes.

Eyelashes she had painstakingly brushed with mascara that very morning because she'd woken up early to look extra pretty.

Eyelashes that were now bleeding that mascara slowly as she began to cry in earnest. Quietly, softly. *With* him.

Rhett pressed the back of his hand to her cheek and brushed the wetness before leaning in. "I'm okay now that I'm back here," he whispered, lifting his other hand to her other cheek and cupping her face gently.

"I guess that makes two of us," she whispered back, closing her eyes and letting go of herself.

She felt the warmth of Rhett's face as it grew nearer to hers, and in that moment, there, at the farm, Maggie had every answer she had ever wanted in her life.

She knew the heartbreak of her mother.

She knew the name of her father.

And she knew her love for Rhett Houston.

So when he pressed his lips against hers, she kissed him back.

And it was a very good choice.

Epilogue

Two Months Later.

Though Rhett had never felt as deep a romantic connection in his life, he respected Maggie's decision to take things slow.

So he started building his own house.

Fortunately, he wouldn't be far—just down off Main Street on a previously empty lot that had long been for sale but had never seen any interest.

He and Maggie had made a deal.

They would date. Formally. Seriously. But they wouldn't live together.

Maggie was a changed woman, she'd said. The sort of woman who didn't live with a man before marriage. Period.

And Rhett, in the wake of his own failed live-in relationship, couldn't agree more. This time, he would do things *right*.

The only way to handle the situation was for Rhett to make a home in Hickory Grove as he'd originally planned. Then, once he and Maggie grew closer and she grew further from the trauma of her "divorce" and the upheaval of the move, they could talk about the next step.

Mainly, that Rhett wanted to propose.

This, of course, was no secret. But he was patient. Patient enough to give Maggie and the kids time to know him better.

Time for them to one day become something of a family. A patchwork family, perhaps, but a family... without rushing. It was for the best.

And anyway, it would be nice for him to have his own space. The barn was a good bachelor pad for the time being, but he was ready to move out and build a new place. A place of his own until it was time to take that next step.

His buddy, Luke, and Maggie's brother, Dirk, (who'd been back in town for a few months during his off-season) pitched in when they could. Rhett hired out when he had to. And Maggie was available to oversee any design choices. But the place was a simple project, by all accounts.

Two bedrooms and one bath.

Open floor plan.

Four walls.

Just enough so that Rhett could sleep there and have small get-togethers. Theo and the guys for football, come fall. Maggie for dinner and a movie. And there was plenty of land for Ky and Dakota to explore. All in all, it was working out better than expected.

And, by late summer, the new house was ready. Or, ready enough for Rhett to move out of the barn.

Gretchen, naturally, was more than thrilled. She was excited to move in behind him and sprawl out. She'd even found the rest of the antique sewing machine she'd been desperately searching for.

Just as soon as Rhett wheeled out the last of his sparse furniture, Gretchen was there, waiting in the wings with Theo, her boxes of books stacked neatly in anticipation of a final resting place.

In fact, Gretchen didn't want to sleep in the barn. Not yet. She was too frightened, she'd said. But she wanted it for her workspace. And, eventually, as a little apartment. Once she got used to the idea of being an adult with her own place. Maybe when she could have someone stay the night with her... eventually.

Now, as the giddy teenager and her dutiful boyfriend stood like sentinels at the barn doors, Maggie helped Rhett lift a side table into the bed of his truck before brushing her hands on her jeans. "I'm going to miss you around here, you know?"

"I'll be just down the road. You can come over whenever you'd like. No need to knock."

She smiled. "Are we still on for dinner?"

"Of course." Rhett slid his hands around the small of her back and brought her in for a discreet kiss.

Maggie accepted it shyly then leaned back. "I'd better go help those two." She hooked a thumb over her shoulder at Gretchen and Theo, who were inside squabbling about where to put the boxes—in the loft for the future or on the floor of the barn where they'd be accessible. "We need to vacuum first!" Maggie hollered.

Rhett smiled and opened his truck door to get in, reaching into his back pocket to remove his phone first.

But it wasn't there.

He strode back toward the open barn door to meet Maggie, who was waving his phone at him, a knowing smirk on her face.

"I *knew* you would find a reason to stick around," she joked, pressing the device to his chest and raising on the balls of her feet to kiss his cheek in a final goodbye. "You left it on the staircase to the loft."

Rhett took the phone and returned her kiss, suddenly wishing he wouldn't be down the road. Or in the barn. Or anywhere else that was a different location from that of the love of his life.

"Thanks," he replied, peeking at the screen before tucking it into his shirt pocket. But as his eyes glanced over the message that was glowing up at him, his face fell. "Oh," he murmured to himself then looked up at Maggie.

"What is it? Is everything okay?"

"It's my sister. Greta," Rhett answered. "I don't know. All she wrote was to call her A.S.A.P."

"Call her," Maggie urged, crossing her arms and frowning.

Rhett did, and Greta answered the phone through sobs.

"Greta, calm down. I can't understand you," Rhett said, meeting Maggie's look of alarm with his own wide eyes.

His little sister sputtered and heaved another sob before coming up for air. "He... he *dumped* me," she said at last, choking on the last two words as if they were poison.

"The tech guy? Your... your *fiancé*? *Kadan*?"

Maggie squeezed her eyes shut in front of him, and he had to look away. Dealing with Greta's love problems made him feel awkward and clumsy.

Greta spat back, "Who else, *Rhett*?"

A grimace took hold of his face and he again looked at Maggie for help. She shrugged and chewed on her lower lip, shaking her head in sorrow on behalf of the poor woman.

"Sorry. I'm sorry, Greta. But, well, *why*?"

Maggie made a face at him and took the phone. "Greta, this is Maggie. Are you okay, sweetheart?"

The two women carried on a brief conversation, Maggie's back turned to Rhett protectively.

After some minutes, she pulled the phone from her ear, tapped the red circle at the bottom, and passed it back to him.

"Well?" Rhett asked, worried for his little sister.

"We're going to get her."

His breathing slowed, as though someone with better wisdom had stepped in to make the right decision. "Okay," he began, ready to help lay out a plan of action. But Maggie turned her head over her shoulder and called out to Gretchen.

"Don't move anything else in there!" She looked back at Rhett, fire in her eyes. "We might have company."

Learn what becomes of Maggie, Rhett, and Greta in *The Innkeeper's House*, the next book in the Hickory Grove series.

Other Titles by Elizabeth Bromke

Birch Harbor:
House on the Harbor
Hickory Grove:
The Schoolhouse
The Christmas House
The Innkeeper's House
Maplewood:
Christmas on Maplewood Mountain
Return to Maplewood
Missing in Maplewood
The Billionaire's Mountain Bride
The Ranger's Mountain Bride
The Cowboy's Mountain Bride

Acknowledgments

A huge thanks to the special people who helped me paint a picture of rural Indiana life and the workings of a farm. Dorothy and Robert Flanagan and Jeanette Engelhard, thank you for your insider knowledge and for taking the time to share your worlds with me. If I've done the farmhouse and barn justice, it's only because of you.

Christina Butrum, I'm so glad to have connected. Your notes and suggestions on fine-tuning were invaluable. I can't wait for Maple Glen! Krissy Moran, thank you for your confidence and validation and, of course, your help with turning a manuscript into a book.

I am so appreciative of Ed, who is not only my partner in life but now also my partner in business. Your perspective and hard work has made all the difference.

A big hug to my family for your patience and support. Without it there is nothing.

Always, I write for my Little E., my muse and my reason.

About the Author

Elizabeth Bromke is the author of the Maplewood series, Hickory Grove series, and Birch Harbor series. In her writing, Bromkes weaves the triumphs and trials of modern relationships. Her settings are rural and notalgic, lending themselves beautifully as backdrops to emotional, heartwarming stories.

In her free time, Elizabeth enjoys reading, walking, and spending time with family. Learn more at elizabethbromke.com today.

Made in the USA
Monee, IL
02 September 2021